Essays in Eighteenth-Century Biography

Essays in Eighteenth-Century Biography

EDITED, WITH AN INTRODUCTION BY

Philip B. Daghlian

INDIANA UNIVERSITY PRESS

BLOOMINGTON AND LONDON

Library of Congress catalog card number: 68-27341

Manufactured in the United States of America

Contents

v

Introduction

PHILIP B. DAGHLIAN / *Indiana University*

The papers in this volume were originally delivered at Indiana University on March 17 and 18, 1967, at a conference on Biography as an Art. They appear essentially in the form in which they were first read, except for the addition of notes and a few minor revisions. The conference, the third on eighteenth-century topics to be held at Indiana, was unusually stimulating. In the following pages I shall attempt to comment briefly on things that were said and to point out other facets of the subject that were not brought up either in the papers or in the ensuing lively discussion. We hope that this volume will help to sustain interest in biography and its problems, especially as applied to the eighteenth century. As a guide to the reader who may wish to pursue the subject further, we conclude the volume with two reference lists. The first is a selective bibliography of studies in eighteenth-century autobiography and biography compiled by Professor Robert E. Kelley of the University of Iowa. The second, a suggested reading list for a course in autobiographical writing of the eighteenth century, is an appendix to Professor Greene's essay.

Although each author received no assignment further than the general topic of Biography as an Art, there was very little overlapping in the papers. Furthermore, the order of presentation turned out to be most appropriate. Professor Rader led off with perhaps the most ambitious paper in scope, since he addresses himself directly to the crucial problem of what makes literature. Professor Greene followed with what is essentially a consideration of the proper materials of biography. Professor Clifford concluded with his treatment of the ethical problem in biography: what and how much should an author tell, and when?

Professor Rader is perfectly right in his contention that some works of history and biography transcend their genres and become literature. His chief illustration of this thesis is Boswell's *Life of Johnson,* one of the preeminent instances of this phenomenon, and his comments demonstrate a close and sympathetic knowledge of the book. Although one may agree fully with the conclusions of the essay, various questions may perhaps be raised about some of Professor Rader's procedures.

He argues that the literary distinction of the *Life* stems from Boswell's vision of the character of Johnson, a vision which controls and governs the use of factual materials in the biography. He proceeds throughout his paper to subject many passages in the book to close literary analysis. He is especially perceptive in his remarks on the dinner with Wilkes, for example. But his concern with strictly literary analysis causes him to put aside a large and highly significant body of material which is certainly relevant. I refer of course to the fact of Boswell as journalist, a topic which sheds a great deal of light on the nature of Boswell's genius.

This aspect of Boswell is so central to him, and has been

expounded with such perception and insight by critics like Professor Pottle and Professor Bronson [1] that it seems almost quixotic of Professor Rader to pass over it in his own discussion. Boswell's journals demonstrate again and again that he possessed a dramatic talent independent of sheer memory. Johnson is his most conspicuous subject, but by no means his only one. None of this contradicts any of Professor Rader's claims in behalf of Boswell the biographer, but his final arguments would seem stronger to one reader, at least, if they included a fuller awareness of Boswell the journalist.

Another point which might have been developed further is the matter of Boswell's image of Johnson. Professor Rader refers to it constantly, and certainly there is no doubt about his assertion that it governs Boswell's choice of incidents and anecdotes. It might have been helpful if Professor Rader had made it clearer that Boswell's "monumental" vision of Johnson was just that, and that it is by no means the only or an inevitable way of considering the subject. Different people see the same object in different ways, but it was this image which loomed largest in Boswell's vision of Johnson.

The major obstacle to immediate acceptance of Professor Greene's plea for paying greater attention to autobiography is his clear dislike of Boswell. As a result one gets some sense from the paper that biography is about to be reduced to a kind of contest between the autobiographer and the biographer. The former is certain to "win" such a contest because the individual subject of a life is likely to know more about himself than another person can. The fact of the matter would seem to be that autobiographical material, when available, is obviously of major importance, but it does not have an automatic and overriding validity, even though every biographer would wish to have access to this kind of material.

Professor Greene's claims for autobiography, that it provides authentic reports on subjective states of mind; that it can record convincingly the minute details of daily life, often of a kind and condition that the external biographer would be unable to find; and that the tone of an autobiographical text can help reveal an author's personality, are all sensible and valid. The danger comes in making them exclusive. Individuals are by no means invariably the soundest judges of their own activities and conditions. An autobiographical narrative may record misapprehension, delusion, or downright error just as easily as unshakable fact. Memory plays tricks on us all. Autobiographical material is important, but only as one class of the materials of the biographer. He will use autobiography whenever he can, but he will use it as part of the larger pattern imposed by all his materials. As a general proposition one might observe that the greater the mass of the autobiographical materials the more difficult and complex the biographer's problems are likely to be. Professor Frederick A. Pottle's *James Boswell: The Earlier Years 1740–1769* (New York, 1966) is a brilliant demonstration of how to treat the problems raised for the biographer by an abundance of autobiographical riches.

A topic touched on in all three essays and yet never dealt with fully is the nature of biographical truth. There is a tendency, most obvious in Professor Greene's remarks, less so in Professor Rader's, and least of all in Professor Clifford's, to assume that there is some kind of "absolute truth" about a person, and that the success of a biography may be evaluated in terms of its degree of attainment of this ideal. Actually, of course, there are many different aspects of any individual's character, and it is one of the primary problems of the biographer to work out his own particular view. To do this he must select details, just the way any artist does, in order to bring out the particular image of biographical truth he perceives. The main difference in this respect between the biographer and the novelist is that the former cannot invent any of the details he uses.

Professor Greene's plea for greater reading of autobiography by students of the eighteenth century (or any other, for that matter) is one I heartily endorse. His appended list of autobiographical works should be most valuable to the reader interested in enlarging his acquaintance in this area. And although the Namierian revolution has pretty well run its course among historians, it is well that literary students of the period should be encouraged to find out more extensively than they now do what people of the time actually said and did and thought.

Not all readers of biography may be concerned with the literary merit of what they read or with the nature of the materials available to the biographer. But most will have a lively interest in the degree of discretion, or the lack of it, reflected in the biography. Professor Clifford's discussion of the ethical problem in biography gives readers plenty to think about. He has studied deeply and thought hard about the problem, with the result that it is not easy to come up with suggestions for further study. But a few observations may be relevant, even though their germs may be found in Profesor Clifford's pages.

One might suggest that the outcry against excessive

revelation by the biographer seems to be related, at least in the later period, to the established opinions about the subject of the life, or, in Professor Clifford's phrase, "the idolatry of the public." If there were something notorious or reprehensible about the subject, the public would be more fascinated than concerned by the biographer's revelation of intimate details. Even in the *Life of Savage* Johnson probably benefitted from the fact that the public tended to expect something verging on the sensational in the life of a figure as romantically notorious as Savage had been. It is typical of Johnson that he should have produced, not a sensational exposé, but rather the honest portrait that he did.

Certainly the second half of the eighteenth century did not lack materials reporting on the more private activities of mankind, to say nothing of womankind. One thinks of the virtually undisguised tête-a-tête portraits in *The Town and Country Magazine,* which kept the public well informed on erotic activity in high life. Or, there were the popular and sensational accounts of trials for Criminal Conversation, which contain similar intelligence, but in more circumstantial detail. No doubt there were many, including at least some of the subjects, who might deplore this kind of publication, but the fact remained that these people had strayed into a realm of notoriety that made them fair game for anyone who came along.

The process seems to have continued to our day. Churchill, Kennedy, and Woodrow Wilson, for example, are all subject to the "idolatry of the public" in varying degrees. Hence the outcries against the books of Lord Moran, William Manchester, and Freud and Bullitt; in each case the kind of revelation in the book tends to diminish the particular aura which posterity (with or without the help of interested parties) seems intent on bestowing on each man. Little concern is expressed, however, when the minute details are about a person with a different kind of aura. There has been no outcry against the kind of gruesome information about the death of Hitler recorded by H. R. Trevor-Roper or Cornelius Ryan.[2] It seems highly probable that the books by Stalin's daughter, as they appear, will contain analagous detail. But since Hitler and Stalin occupy different niches in history than do Churchill, Kennedy, or Woodrow Wilson, there has been no outcry, nor is one likely.

Professor Clifford reminds us that the charges of breach of decorum against Boswell were exactly of the kind recently made against Mr. Manchester. One can suggest that the outcry against a book is not likely to last very long. Already Lord Moran has receded pretty much into the background, even though his book has a firm place in the corpus of essential information about Churchill. A good book survives the temporary complaints that may develop; a bad book may even survive a little longer than it might otherwise, just because of such publicity. But long-term survival is going to depend, as it always has, on the degree of truth which the book communicates. If this present volume does nothing else, it should remind the reader that biographical truth is a very subtle and complicated entity, but that the biographer has the same problems that the novelist or the poet ultimately has, to order experience concretely and memorably.

Acknowledgments

The contributors to this volume, Professors Clifford, Greene, Kelley, and Rader, have been most cooperative in the complicated process of assembling a book by mail. They have observed deadlines and their copy has arrived in usable form. For such courtesies I am grateful. We are all additionally grateful to Professor Clifford for his valuable suggestions and advice during the planning of this book. For various kinds of aid and counsel on the local scene I thank my colleagues Howard Anderson, William R. Cagle, and Ronald Gottesman.

P.B.D.

Bloomington, Indiana
August 30, 1967

Essays in Eighteenth-Century Biography

Literary Form in Factual Narrative: The Example of Boswell's *Johnson* [1]

RALPH W. RADER / University of California at Berkeley

Although factual narrative, that is to say, history and biography, is certainly an art, only a few biographies and histories are unequivocally literature. This paradox deserves explanation and will in fact provide the whole subject of my remarks in this chapter. While much biography and history has a clear if relatively low place in literature, only Boswell and Gibbon in English have constructed factual narratives which stand unquestioned as literary masterpieces of the very first rank. On the other hand, much excellent biography and history has no place in literature at all. The explanation for these facts lies in the fundamental contrast between the fictional and the factual narrative modes. Literature in general is, in Coleridge's phrase, that species of composition which proposes pleasure rather than truth as its immediate object. The purely literary artist is free to invent, dispose, weight, and vivify his materials as a means to the greatest intensity of effect, whereas the immediate object of the biographer or historian cannot be effect but fidelity to truth.

Some works of history and biography nevertheless produce a distinct and powerful effect closely akin to those

3

which characterize works of the imagination, and these of course are, as they should be from Coleridge's definition, the very works which rank as literature.

But though we speak of Gibbon's epical sweep and force and Macaulay's dramatic powers, we ought not to succumb to the temptations of analogy and talk as if the *Decline and Fall* were in fact an epic, or the *History of England* a drama, or even as if the most celebrated contemporary work of factual narrative is what its author calls it, a non-fiction novel. To do so would be to evade the terms of the question we want to answer, which is, not how literary works are literary, but how works whose primary commitment is distinctly non-literary nevertheless become literature.

The answer which I am going to propose is that such works become literature by transcending while fulfilling the usual purpose of history and biography, to provide true knowledge of the human past. I am going to suggest that factual narratives in order to compass a literary effect must raise their subjects constructively out of the past and represent them to the imagination as concrete, self-intelligible causes of emotion. My claim will be that these works of history thereby become, paradoxically, "a more philosophical and a higher thing than history." They become universal, in Aristotle's sense, because they are displayed to the imagination not as contingent but as concretely probable, and valuable in terms of that general human nature which as human beings we all share and intuitively know. I choose as my text Boswell's *Life of Johnson* but shall return intermittently and at the close to a view of the overall subject.

It has not been obvious to the authors of the two most

extensive and scholarly modern treatments of biography that the greatest work of factual narrative in our language has a structure which is the cause of its greatness, and that effective structure, as all writers should know, is never an accident. Donald Stauffer, though he gives high praise to Boswell's artistry, says flatly that "the structure of the *Life* is open to serious question." It lacks narrative connection and temporal development, it fails to scale itself to the proportions of Johnson's life, and (astoundingly) it fails to create Johnson, affording rather "materials from which Johnson may be created by an imaginative act." [2] John Garraty repeats the charges and adds a few of his own: the book is "all out of proportion"; it is merely "one man's recollections of another"; it lacks "not so much unity as cumulative effect and a comprehensive estimate of its subject and his importance." [3] As we shall see, it would make as much sense to blame Shakespeare for not providing a comprehensive estimate of Hamlet. Most of these criticisms point to real facts about the substance and structure of the *Life,* but they do not point to faults. Only the inadequate theoretical conception which underlies the criticism could make these facts seem faults, for no reader intuitively reacts to them as such. The problem lies in conceiving Boswell's work as if it were an ordinary explanatory narrative, like Krutch's biography of Johnson. If it were such a biography, then it would be a manifestly defective one, and we should have to pronounce it inferior to Krutch's. This would be absurd, for fine as it is, Krutch's biography is not great literature and Boswell's is. That is the whole point. It is literature. It is not an explanatory narrative but an emotive narrative of the type we have indicated, one whose whole principle is not to give instrumental information and explanation but rather to reconstruct and present as concrete and universal an aspect of human fact so as to render it inherently the cause of a distinct effect. What aspect of fact does Boswell reconstruct, and what is its effect? The answer lies in the last sentence of his book: "Such was Samuel Johnson, a man whose talents, acquirements, and virtues were so extraordinary, that the more his character is considered, the more he will be regarded by the present age and by posterity, with admiration and reverence." The subject of Boswell's book is not the life of Johnson but the *character* of Johnson as revealed in the facts of his life; and his purpose is to make us feel that admiration and reverence which is the natural emotive consequence of full empathetic perception of the character.

Unlike Scott's life, Johnson's career as a connected sequence of actions could not have been presented as the cause of a powerful effect. It is his character alone—the extraordinary strength, subtlety, and depth of his mental powers, joined with the nobility and magnanimity of his moral nature and his astonishing powers of expression—that contains the potentiality of such an effect. This Boswell knew. That concluding sentence is no accident, nor is the brilliant character sketch which precedes it and pulls together into a single retrospective view the subject which the myriad pieces of his book have together evoked.

Character must be manifested in the concrete, and Johnson's character is known primarily from its concrete manifestation in the *Life*. Just because the concrete is or seems to be a given reality, however, Boswell has gained small credit for showing it to us. So discerning a critic as Joseph Wood Krutch can see Boswell's technique as wholly naturalistic: "What he [needs is] not imagination or insight, or even, primarily, the judgment to select. It is documentation and more documentation." [4] The well-known, often answered, but still recurring charge that Boswell was nothing but a tape recorder is a ghost that ought to be permanently laid, but it will continue to haunt us until we perceive with more clarity and certainty than we yet have that Boswell's book is, in the part and in the whole, not a recording of fact but always and everywhere an implicitly affecting artistic selection and construction of an aspect of fact. George Mallory pointed out long ago that the effect of the *Life* does not depend on its factuality but upon Boswell's power of "picking out [from the facts] all that was characteristic and important, of ruthlessly discarding unnecessary details and presenting only the salient points." "He gives not the whole of Johnson's words but the essence of them," preserving only "the spirit [and, we may add, the effect] of Johnson's talk and the atmosphere of the moment as the listeners felt it." The talk is "too deliberate, too close, too well-winnowed, as it were" to be a transcript of the actual. The effect of Boswell's operation on the facts, Mallory nevertheless concludes, was to make the whole more real, "a better representation of Johnson." [5]

All this implies the creative secret of Boswell's art: he had within his mind not a series of disjunctive photographic impressions but a single dynamic image of Johnson which, though it derived from innumerable manifestations of Johnson's character, was nevertheless quite independent of any particular manifestation and even independent of their sum. He knew Johnson's image mimetically, and he knew it in its essence. We remember that he could impersonate Johnson more vividly and exactly than Garrick, giving something that approached a full psychosomatic impression. We remember that he could make fresh Johnsoniana, with the ring of the true coin: "Dine with Jack Wilkes, Sir! I'd as soon dine with Jack Ketch!" But just because he possessed Johnson's image so completely within himself, he knew its value immediately and fully through the involuntary psychic comparison with himself which the act of mimetic participation implied. In Johnson's presence Boswell always felt an intense exhilaration as he imaginatively participated in Johnson's powers. It is easy to understand how in retrospect that exhilaration became an unshakable reverence and admiration.

In creating the *Life,* then, Boswell was in a real sense creating an objective correlative of a grand emotive idea. His idea was not so much an aid to him in his task as it was the very principle of that astonishing reconstruction. No other assumption can account for the fact, indicated by Mallory and others, that the Johnson of the *Life* is more Johnsonian than Johnson himself could invariably be. To breathe life into the concentrated dust of the notes and to shape from them the form of the living Johnson can in no sense be conceived as a mechanical act directed toward a string of discrete memories but only as a fully organic act of the creative imagination.[6] Boswell had not to record dead memories but to construct a re-enactment of Johnson which would be concretely adequate in itself to reproduce and release in the reader the emotion which the living man had once produced in him. And the fullest proof of the truly imaginative nature of his act is that he found the correlative of his idea not only in the facts which he himself had witnessed but in all the other facts which his industry had brought to light. His book, he says, is made up of "innumerable detached particulars," but it is not therefore a melange; the particulars are not a heterogeneous collection of facts but a homogeneous presentation of character. Each of the particulars is displayed by Boswell, to the degree which each inherently permits, as an epiphany of an infinitely varied but always single character. Boswell's image of Johnson is the selective, constructive, and controlling principle of the *Life*, the omnipresent element which vivifies and is made vivid in the whole. The image is the unity—the real and living unity—of the *Life*.

It is obvious therefore why the book lacks narrative connection and temporal development. The uniqueness of Johnson's character manifested itself in moments of time and not over a temporal sequence. There is no external connection of parts in the *Life* because the subject can be expressed only as the essence of its individual manifestations; there is no development because the character *in its uniqueness* was static. It is obvious also why the book is not scaled to the proportions of the actual life: more facts expressive of character were available from the late than from the early life.

The creative and unifying role which Boswell's internalized idea of Johnson plays in the *Life* can be forcefully demonstrated from his treatment of those portions of the life in which he himself had played no part. Critics have not sufficiently noticed the very many occasions when Boswell shows his dramatic talent quite independent of his memory. One recalls, for example, the vivid and pleasing scene where Langton and Beauclerk rouse a comically formidable Johnson in the middle of the night and take him on a midnight frisk. It is alive before us; yet Boswell was a boy in Edinburgh when it occurred. How many such scenes in the *Life* Boswell never saw but makes the reader see because he saw them not in reality but where the true artist always sees—in the mind's eye. But of the parts in which Boswell's memory played no part, the most instructive for our present purpose are those which may be compared with parallel parts from the works of Boswell's rivals, Hawkins and Mrs. Piozzi. Neither of those writers, of course, was moved by any detached sense of Johnson's magnificent mystery to discover every possible sign of it; they were content with what lay at hand. The very immensity of Boswell's *Life* is itself evidence, in comparison with their works, of the way in which he was possessed by the essence of his subject and motivated to give it body. They were prompted to write about a particular man whom they had known, from private emotion; Boswell was driven to write about a man who was intrinsically of interest to all men, by disinterested universal emotion. Both Hawkins and Mrs. Piozzi held and expressed the same general estimate of Johnson that Boswell does—he was an astonishingly great and good man—but neither is consistently able to show us the materials of their works as the cause of their estimate. Too often, they allow merely personal feeling to interfere with their presentation of the universal Johnson. Consider the following anecdote told by both Boswell and Mrs. Piozzi. Boswell first: "In the playhouse at Lichfield, as Mr. Garrick informed me, Johnson having for a moment quitted a chair which was placed for him between the side-scenes, a gentleman took possession of it, and when Johnson on his return civilly demanded his seat, rudely refused to give it up; upon which Johnson laid hold of it, and tossed him and the chair into the pit." [7] Mrs. Piozzi's version is as follows: Garrick "said that in their young days, when some strolling players came to Lichfield, our friend had fixed his place upon the stage, and got himself a chair accordingly; which leaving a few minutes, he found a man in it at his return, who refused to give it back at the first intreaty: Mr. Johnson, however, who did not think it worth his while to make a second, took chair and man and all together and threw them all at once into the pit." [8] There is a good deal of difference in precision and elegance of narration here, of course; Boswell's is much the shorter, with no irrelevant detail, the whole laid out in the clean curve of a single sentence. And Boswell's works together with a series of short epiphanies he is giving at the moment to illustrate his nicely discriminated immediate thesis that Johnson was afraid of nothing but death, not even what might occasion death. But the most basic difference is that Boswell's version in itself supports his claim that Johnson was a great and good man. Mrs. Piozzi's does not support her claim and thereby fails to display that which she has pointed to as the natural interest of her subject. The choice which she made in evaluating Garrick's story was as a personal moral choice just as justifiable as Boswell's, but as an artistic choice, it was not defensible at all, since it diminished the inherent potential of the subject. If Johnson had been as she shows him here, we would feel no interest and take no pleasure in reading about him. Mrs. Piozzi's mistake was repeated, on a much larger scale, by a much greater biographer—Froude, in his *Life of Carlyle*.

There is an example of parallel tendency in Hawkins,

who writes thus of a famous incident at Oxford: Johnson had "scarce any change of raiment, and, in a short time after Corbet left him, but one pair of shoes, and those so old, that his feet were seen through them: a gentleman of his college, the father of an eminent clergyman now living, directed a servitor one morning to place a new pair at the door of Johnson's chamber, who, seeing them upon his first going out, so far forgot himself and the spirit that must have actuated his unknown benefactor, that, with all the indignation of an insulted man, he threw them away." [9] The essential facts are as Boswell is to present them: the shoes were given and Johnson was indignant. The problem is in evaluation: it was a fault in Johnson to be indignant. It may be true; yet in judging Johnson on a narrow moral base Hawkins diminishes him. Johnson is seen to fall away from a universal standard of virtue and to become by that much less the man because of whose greatness Hawkins is writing. Boswell, without at all changing the facts, reads and relates them in a much different way: "Mr. Bateman's lectures were so excellent, that Johnson used to come and get them at second-hand from Taylor, till his poverty being so extreme, that his shoes were worn out, and his feet appeared through them, he saw that this humiliating circumstance was perceived by the Christ-Church men, and he came no more. He was too proud to accept of money, and somebody having set a pair of new shoes at his door, he threw them away with indignation. How must we feel when we read such an anecdote of Samuel Johnson!" [10] Hawkins' inert details and judgments drop out as Boswell makes us feel Johnson's poverty and the reality of his consequent humiliation. Boswell construed his pride convincingly as a sign of his majestic independ-

ence, and, suppressing the irrelevant clergyman, evaluates
the incident not in relation to him but to Johnson's essential character and the fact of his permanent greatness,
something to which Bateman's excellent lectures and Johnson's desire for them are not of course irrelevant. Critics
often seem to assume that the Boswellian record is superior
to the Hawkins and Piozzi record largely in its greater
material fullness: there is more documentation. If this
were true, then it would have been no literary crime for
Croker to have conflated as he did all three works together; facts are facts. But it *was* a crime because the records are different not in extent but, as Professor Clifford
has seen, in their fundamental nature.[11] Boswell's facts are
created according to the model of a living universal idea
of a great man, the minor biographers' as impressions of
the contingent acts of a contingent man who sometimes
displayed his greatness.

(The passage quoted from Hawkins, incidentally, wit-
nesses to an interesting point. In attempting to impose
universal moral judgment on Johnson's imperfect action,
Hawkins is imitating Johnson's own biographical practice,
just as he attempted to imitate Johnson's style. Johnson
succeeds in his biographies because he genuinely does
impose his judgment on the facts. His biographies are
literature because they achieve universality of judgment,
not because they display the inherent universality of their
subject. The pleasure of Johnson's *Lives* is Johnson, not
Pope or Addison. This shows how untrue is the usual
statement that Boswell followed Johnson's biographical
example. He followed it in its emphasis on character and
on characterizing particularity, but he departed totally
from the basic Johnsonian mode of presentation. John-

son's practice, of course, was ideally suited to his gifts, for the same reasons that made him the ideal subject for Boswell's kind of biography.)

Once the nature of Boswell's image of Johnson has been pointed out, its presence and constructive function are everywhere apparent. Many facts in the *Life,* however, would not in themselves contribute directly to our vivid sense of the character, and it is not immediately clear why they should have been included if the subject of the work is as I describe it. Briefly we may say that Boswell treats the full range of facts in the life on the assumption, amply born out by modern scholars, that anything connected with such a man will contribute a little bit more to our attempt to fill out and confirm the inherently fascinating reality of his image. In factual literature, we *do* want to know how many children had Lady Macbeth. But Boswell, as may easily be illustrated, always proportions his treatment of a fact to the relevance it has for the image of essential character, so that he dismisses quickly much that has great importance in the progress of Johnson's life and devotes pages to what does not affect its progress at all. He explains the substantive biographical facts adequately as facts but always in such a way as to shape and control their significance as emblems of the admirable character. Take, for instance, Boswell's account of Johnson's pension.[12] We see at once that it is not an account of a fact in itself but a transformation of a potentially hostile fact into the terms of the image. He begins by placing the grant in the glowing context of George III's liberal and disinterested patronage and only then contemptuously characterizes the charges of venality which had been made against Johnson. He then refutes the charges by a detailed citation of wit-nesses, painstakingly and concretely recreating the motivation on both sides, and emerges with the dramatically won conclusion that the pension had been granted on "liberal and honourable terms." The passage closes with Johnson's nobly dignified letter to Bute, which concretely confirms and amplifies the judgment Boswell has offered, so that the reader is left secure in truth and admiration, the image not only intact but fortified. Examples of such essay-parts, as we may call them, clearly shaped to the large end of the book, could be multiplied.

But the fact that the shaping role of Boswell's grand image of Johnson is especially obvious in particular passages should not prevent our perceiving its active presence in every part of the *Life*. We hear it vibrate in the fanfare of the very first sentence: "To write the Life of him who excelled all mankind in writing the lives of others, and who, whether we consider his extraordinary endowments, or his various works, has been equalled by few in any age, is an arduous, and may be reckoned in me a presumptuous task." A grand and confident claim has been made upon our attention. We necessarily infer that the claim has a cause in reality external to the narrator, and we respond as to a perceived fact with a corresponding mental and emotional assumption of our own. The narrative posture thereafter continuously asserts the real existence of the image thus evoked and continues to demand its counterpart in us. Thus, even when the facts immediately produced do not actively validate the image, the reader never doubts its reality because the narrator does not evaluate such facts as validation but only as necessarily interesting and relevant, in relation to the curiosity which the continuing image naturally generates.

More than narrative assertion is required, of course, to call Johnson's spirit from the vasty deep, particularly in the opening pages where so little of the concrete is available; and the discerning critic can only admire the many subtle means Boswell employs to bring the permanent Johnson quickly before us. In the facts of the youth he discovers the greatness of the man; and with the voice of the man he makes the youth vivid. He selects, compresses, dramatizes, vivifies to such a degree that when at last the figure of Johnson walks through Davies' doorway, he is an old and beloved acquaintance.

More largely, throughout the *Life,* many subtle features, quite distinct from its factual substance, conspire to renew and intensify our sense of the grandeur of the subject. Recurring epithets like "my illustrious friend" give us a tug of pleasure and reanimate our established estimate as we think subconsciously, "he *was* illustrious." Even such apparently irrelevant aspects of the book as its praise of great men, or its literary allusions, or Boswell's digression on the qualities of a noble estate contribute in the aggregate to the massive special effect of the whole. (Only consider how much grander and more spacious is the world of the *Life* than the world of Boswell's *London Journal.*)

In a moment I shall pay detailed attention to the means by which the image is given redundant concrete specification, but I should not leave the subject of the peripheral means Boswell employs in connection with it without noticing two directly related matters, his citation of the testimony of others and his use of Johnson's letters. Both these dimensions of his work serve as necessary guarantees that we are encountering not a personal but a universal view of the subject. The testimony of others validates and extends the view Boswell himself takes; and the letters, each of which, as Professor Daghlian has recently noted, powerfully images Johnson's noble character,[13] offer the strongest possible objective corroboration of the image: the Johnson we meet in the letters is indubitably the same as the Johnson Boswell elsewhere shows us. From all this we understand how the image becomes a covert but omnipresent reality in the *Life,* even in those facts which in themselves would not evoke it. The explanation offered here as confirmed by the actual experience of a continuous reading of the *Life* allows us to understand how such seemingly inert facts are drawn into relevance by the unseen lines of magnetic force which the large image and emotional flow of the whole exert and how each functions as one of the myriad particles which together make the lines real and distinct. The image constructs the facts, and the facts in turn construct the image; the process, circular and progressive, constitutes the linear coherence and material unity of the *Life.*

But unity and coherence do not by themselves make literature. To understand why the *Life* is a supremely literary work, we must explain its power, unmatched among factual narratives, of producing literary pleasure. The explanation lies in the unusual degree to which the *Life* is able, within the limits of truth, to meet Coleridge's supplementary requirement that literary works ought to be so designed as to give in each of their parts as much pleasure as is consonant with the greatest pleasure in the whole. Lockhart's *Life of Scott,* for instance, has a plot-like structure, a single line of developing tragic perception, which produces a powerful single effect, but the constituent parts are relatively inert. As a whole, consequently, it is much less a work of literature than Boswell's. The *Life of Johnson* gives maximum pleasure just because it is so preponderantly made up of images of Johnson's acts, each of which has its own particular pleasure which, when most fully realized, most contributes to the peculiar pleasure of the whole. To understand this, we must remember what Aristotle teaches: that literary pleasure results from the vivid representation to our consciousness of striking human acts, morally determinate, which move us through our perception of the internal probability and ethical consonance of their inception, continuance, and completion. Now, as I shall more fully illustrate, all the acts in the *Life* are represented according to this formula. Boswell renders them vivid and striking, makes us see them as internally probable in terms of motive and circumstance, and adjusts our view so that we always see them as ethically consonant both in themselves and with the morally determinate image of an admirable Johnson. Each of the representational parts, then, has its own local pleasure, but the parts are of such a nature that in sum they also form the basis of the larger literary pleasure of the entire book—the single continuing, growing and self-reinforcing pleasure of encountering in new and striking but always probable manifestations the astonishing character of Samuel Johnson. That we know these new manifestations as probable and encounter them with anticipatory pleasure demonstrates the fact that the image, though it has no single material expression, nonetheless exists as an active essence in the reader's mind which, as I have already said, effectively renders even the inert parts concrete. (That we possess the liberated image of Johnson even after the fact of reading the *Life* is demonstrated by the effect upon us of the words

"Sir" or "Why, No Sir" spoken out of context but with appropriate inflection. The utterance immediately brings to mind that amusing but admirable conjunction of sincere deference and rational aggression which together reflect the essence of Johnson's character. A similar phenomenon obtains for no other historical figure.)

It may help to clarify the large structural principle of the *Life* if we recall that we have already seen it in action in the episodes compared with their counterparts in Hawkins and Mrs. Piozzi. When Boswell's Johnson throws the interloper off the stage, we are made to see his action as ethically consonant with, though conventionally disproportionate to, the provocation he has received and his own dignity, so that the scene becomes comically pleasing; at the same time, Johnson's overall moral stature is pleasurably confirmed and reinforced. Mrs. Piozzi's Johnson, by contrast, is neither amusing nor admirable. When Boswell's Johnson throws away the shoes at Oxford, we are moved by a momentary pulse of admiring compassion, because we understand the grounds of his act fully and evaluate it as justified; at the same time, we see a permanently grand aspect of his nature. Hawkins' Johnson is shown to neither purpose.

But Coleridge's principle about the relation of parts to the whole has in view not only such material parts as episodes in a representation but also purely qualitative parts. The pleasure of any literary work will increase in proportion as all its elements, including those of language itself—syntax, diction, and pure sound—are arranged so as actively to support the effect. For example, other things being equal, a representation in verse is more intensely pleasing than one in prose. Here, then, is another cause of the supreme literary quality of the *Life*. Johnson's speech —edited and pointed by Boswell to preserve and heighten its Johnsonian essence—makes him the only character in factual literature whose speech is equal to or superior to that of fictional characters. The graceful elasticity and full vital expressiveness of Boswell's own purposefully unobtrusive style work toward the same end to make the *Life* unique as a factual work which to the large pleasure of concrete character and the smaller pleasure of concrete act can add the fully perfecting concrete pleasures of language itself. (At least once in the *Life* we get the pleasure of speech as a pure increment to the already forceful sense: "He seemed to take pleasure in speaking in his own style," says Boswell; "for when he had carelessly missed it, he would repeat the thought translated into it. Talking of the Comedy of 'The Rehearsal,' he said, 'It has not wit enough to keep it sweet.' This was easy; he therefore caught himself, and pronounced a more rounded sentence; 'It has not vitality enough to preserve it from putrefaction.' " [14] Pure style, pure pleasure—but as always in Johnson, the style is the man.)

But the vital corpuscles of the *Life's* body are the acts. Let us take them first at their simplest and then at their most complex. The simplest kind of complete act represented in the *Life* is an aphorism or generalization by Johnson without context. Now any general truth even independent of a speaker has a representational character and force: the mind perceives it as a self-caused, inherently purposeful, surprising but probable act of cognition, carrying with it therefore its own distinct pleasure. The pleasure of a generalization will be greater in proportion to the degree in which it is both true and unobvious, to the inherent human relevance of its substance, and to the concision and force of its expression. To describe the conditions of pleasure in generalizations is to suggest the qualities of Johnson's. As much as La Rochefoucauld's and Pascal's, Johnson's sayings have literary value in and of themselves, with the additional pleasure of their spontaneity; it is not too much to say that the recorded impromptus of all other men together do not equal the total of his in pleasure and value. Yet all of his remarks in the *Life* give additional pleasure, on the large grounds sketched out above, in that they satisfy as fresh but unforeseeable signs of the power of the character and at the same time add an increment to the total pleasurable image. Let us take one of the myriad examples, the statement, "All censure of a man's self is oblique praise. It is in order to show how much he can spare. It has all the invidiousness of self-praise, and all the reproach of falsehood." [15] The initial sentence, paradoxical and surprising, is quickly and pleasingly rendered inherently probable (that is, true) by the explanatory second sentence. The compelling analytic judgment of the third sentence converts what might have been a cynicism of La Rochefoucauld's into an implicit positive base of moral operations. It is not directed scornfully at *other* men but put instructively, for the use of *all* men, including the speaker. The statement surprises, pleases, and teaches; and it leaves the mind with a renewed and augmented sense of the simultaneously good, wise, and articulate man who made it. But even when Johnson's statements are perfectly particular they are pleasurable merely as fresh revelations of the established admirable character. "Sir, I would walk to the extent of the diameter of the earth to save Beauclerk."

Or: "Sir, you have not travelled over *my* mind, I promise you." [16] Notice that the hyperbolical first statement would not please if our conviction of Johnson's majestic rectitude and the depth of his feeling did not give it substance; and that the second, if said by Goldsmith to Johnson, rather than the other way around, would be merely an egotistical impertinence.

But the most massively pleasing parts of the *Life* are its scenes. The art of the major scenes is so plain that they have often drawn praise upon Boswell for the vividness of their pointing and their parenthetical stage directions ["Johnson (puffing and blowing): . . ."]. But these praises are often analytically empty because the critics who give them have no conception of the form and effect to which the devices are subordinate. After "vivid" and "dramatic" there is nothing left. Space does not permit me to work in full detail through the most famous scene in the *Life,* the Wilkes episode,[17] but a partial analysis can sufficiently demonstrate how much its effect depends upon Boswell's handling. Its essential structure may be described by expanding the basic formula already set down: it is a full Aristotelian action which follows the predicament of a central character from a beginning which defines the terms of that predicament, through a middle which develops and complicates it and our reactions to the full, to an end which resolves the complications and brings our emotional participation to satisfactory discharge and close. More particularly, it is a comic action. Now in a comic action the hero is of mixed character—essentially and predominantly good, so that we wish him finally well; at the same time flawed or restricted in a way that involves him in embarrassments which are the substance of the complications of the plot. We view these embarrassments with delight both because they are of the hero's own making and because the conduct of the story assures us throughout that he will in some way that our perplexity cannot foresee ultimately achieve the due which his fundamentally good character deserves and that meanwhile nothing really harmful or painful will befall him.[18] Boswell shows us the Wilkes episode according to just this formula.

At the outset, Johnson is already secure in our admiration, but Boswell must make us actively desire to see a kind of trick played on him. He does this initially by making us feel that the meeting will be a delightful experiment in human nature which will end much to the Doctor's credit and by heightening our sense of that awful personal power in Johnson which by itself guarantees the preservation of his dignity while it enhances our comic sense of Boswell's resourceful daring. ("How to manage it, was a nice and difficult matter.") Boswell sets the terms of the story by defining Johnson and Wilkes as "celebrated men" who, though as different as they could possibly be, are yet both friends of Boswell. The meeting is thus neatly characterized as potentially productive either of an explosion or a conciliation. We are made to feel that the last will and ought to be the result but are left to wonder how, considering Johnson's strong moral and political prejudices, the first will be avoided. The terms are quickly sharpened with the apparently gratuitous paragraph about Sir John Pringle who, like Wilkes, was also linked to Johnson through the middle term of Boswell's friendship but who, though an excellent man, was "not sufficiently flexible" to meet agreeably with him. The paragraph has a very precise function: it underlines the potential explo-

siveness of the desired meeting and Boswell's own underlying assurance that the explosion will somehow not
occur, while at the same time it defines any inflexibility
which might stand in its way as a regrettable human
limitation. From this point on, therefore, the reader must
actively hope that Johnson will be able to meet Wilkes
on affable terms, while he is all the more aware of the
piquant difficulties.

The paragraph on arrangements with Dilly increases
with every detail our sense of the necessity that Johnson
for his own sake meet the standards of social sophistication, while Dilly's represented alarm reinforces our sense
of the internal barrier to his doing so. The next scene
shows Boswell with consummate meekness and guile in-
ducing Johnson to accept the invitation through a subtle
challenge to his vanity as a social man. The paragraph
could sustain a page of analysis, but I will only say that
its brilliance consists in Boswell's heightening our comic
sense of Johnson's majestically cantankerous nature at the
same time that he makes us sympathetic to Johnson's full
if inadvertent commitment of his pride to the fact that he
is not ultimately limited by his prickliness. "And if Jack
Wilkes *should* be there, what is that to *me*, Sir?" Johnson
must make good this commitment, but all the more we
wonder: how is he to do it?

The obstacle presented by Mrs. Williams is used fully
by Boswell to heighten by opposing the wishes we have
formed to see the meeting take place, as well as for other
purposes; and when the obstacle is overcome we exult
with Boswell as his prize is carried off. Snug and silent,
we watch with delight the impact upon Johnson of Mr.
Arthur Lee and then Mr. Wilkes. Boswell defines Lee's

comic function with brilliant economy by juxtaposing a description of him in the idiom of Johnson's prejudice— he was both a "patriot" and an "American"—with a comment that underlines his membership in the civilized world of which we desire Johnson to be fully a member—Lee was, Boswell says, later American ambassador to the Court of Madrid. In other words, we see Lee at once as Johnson in his comic limitation sees him and also as he really is and as Johnson must therefore finally accept him if he is to maintain and increase our regard. But just at this moment we are most aware of the resources it will require in Johnson to overcome the strength of his prejudice as Boswell vividly communicates his comic distress—"too, too, too." The distress is visible, but if the effect is to be maintained, we need as well some assurance that the hoped for if as yet unspecifiable triumph will eventually come and that it will come not accidentally but as a result of Johnson's deliberate attempt to master himself and the situation. No sign is available, and so Boswell boldly goes into Johnson's mind to get it for us: "His feelings, *I dare say,* were awkward enough. But he *no doubt* recollected his having rated me for supposing that he could be at all disconcerted by any company, and he, *therefore,* resolutely set himself to behave quite as an easy man of the world, who could adapt himself at once to the disposition and manners of those whom he might chance to meet." The sympathetic vanity and our hopes for its triumph are strong in our minds.

Despite his resolution, Johnson's "surly virtue" is shown to yield only gradually as the conciliatory gestures of the suave but sincere Wilkes make us wish all the more for Johnson's triumph of sophistication. All the matter now heightens and foreshadows the climax, in ways we cannot pause to notice, until we get the climactic interchange: "JOHNSON. (to Mr. Wilkes) 'You must know, Sir, I lately took my friend Boswell and shewed him genuine civilised life in an English provincial town. I turned him loose at Lichfield, my native city, that he might see for once real civility: for you know he lives among savages in Scotland, and among rakes in London.' WILKES. 'Except when he is with grave, sober, decent people like you and me.' JOHNSON. (smiling). 'And we ashamed of him.' " The speeches please not just in themselves but because they resolve with such unexpected and delightful fulness the underlying tensions which have been so clearly and vividly represented from the outset. Johnson's first speech—"and rakes in London"—covertly and politely acknowledges and thus neutralizes the antagonism which he has felt toward Wilkes and which has been the source of our comic concern. Wilkes, just as politely, denies any antagonism by defining himself with Johnson as among the "grave, sober, decent people"—the three adjectives are a giveaway —as opposed to the rakes. Johnson's smiling "And we ashamed of him" accepts the denial, cancels the animosity, joins himself to Wilkes, and, in a complete reversal of the original terms of the incident, leaves the Boswell who had challenged Johnson's civility comically out in the social cold, a barbarous Scot. The single adjective, "smiling," applied to Johnson is, of course, not just a piece of random vividness but is crucially important to our full sense of the active benevolence with which Johnson reconciles himself to Wilkes; it is not the limited triumph of self-control over ineradicable and debilitating prejudice, but the full-hearted triumph of a capaciously human soul whose prejudice is only a temporary defect of its large virtues. It should be clear even from this brief analysis that the pleasurable effect not only of the climax but of the whole depends on the facts *only* as they are selected, revealed and evaluated by Boswell's art.

The interchange does not end the episode, but we cannot pause to follow Boswell's means of bringing it to full aesthetic completeness. Enough has been said to show how the episode, like the other parts we have examined, makes its fullest contribution to the overall purpose of the *Life* when its own appropriate pleasure is most realized. The inherent particular effect of the Wilkes episode is comic pleasure, and that pleasure has been seen to increase in proportion to Johnson's triumph. The greater, the more surprising, and yet characteristically probable the triumph, the greater the comic pleasure. But obviously then the greater the comic pleasure, the greater our residual admiration for Johnson. We should notice, too, that the episode necessarily depends on the preceding part of the *Life*, for an active idea of Johnson's character is a requisite of its comic effect. No one who reads the episode without experience of the *Life* will think it very funny.

A great part of the pleasure of the scenes taken as a whole is their wide range of effect from somberness to the gayest lightness, while all express the same Johnson and all are indebted to Boswell's art. Consider, for instance, the grand scene where Boswell introduces "the subject of death, and [endeavors] to maintain that the fear of it might be got over." [19] The conversation must have lasted some time but Boswell gives only its heart. Johnson's

defense of his own fear of death as against the alleged
lack of fear in Hume and Foote justifies him immediately
in our estimation because he finds evidence for his own
feelings that we cannot deny: "Hold a pistol to Foote's
breast, or to Hume's breast, and threaten to kill them,
and you'll see how they behave." Still, we would not be
really prepared to absorb the gigantic outburst which follows Boswell's "But may we not fortify our minds for the
approach of death?" if Boswell had not been able, without
breaking the rhythm of the scene, to specify and ennoble
Johnson's inner state:

I am sensible I was in the wrong, to bring before his view what
he ever looked upon with horrour; for although when in a
celestial frame, in his "Vanity of human wishes," he has supposed death to be "kind Nature's signal for retreat," from
this state of being to "a happier seat," his thoughts upon this
aweful change were in general full of dismal apprehensions.
His mind resembled the vast amphitheatre, the Coliseum at
Rome. In the centre stood his judgement, which, like a mighty
gladiator, combated those apprehensions that, like the wild
beasts of the *Arena,* were all around in cells, ready to be let
out upon him. After a conflict, he drove them back into their
dens; but not killing them, they were still assailing him. To
my question, whether we might not fortify our minds for the
approach of death, he answered, in a passion, "No, Sir, let it
alone. It matters not how a man dies, but how he lives. The
act of dying is not of importance, it lasts so short a time."
He added, (with an earnest look) "A man knows it must be
so, and submits. It will do him no good to whine."

Boswell's grand simile, though necessary, is dangerous.
Were it not for its manifest accuracy and truth and its
immediate validation by the grandeur of Johnson's reply,

so artificial a comparison could easily have been a disaster. But it succeeds by forcing us to understand that Johnson's unusual fear of death does not diminish him, since it makes us feel how constant and tremendous the pressures upon him were, how great was the effort needed to hold them in equilibrium, and how near to breaking without ever really breaking his majestic nature was. The agitated but noble reply confirms all this and releases Johnson from the blame of personal defect because, though it functions fully as the sign to us of his particular emotion, it is perfectly general and fully applicable to all other human beings, so that we see him not as a particular fearful man but as an exemplar of the most basic kind of human heroism. Our sense of the splendid agony of his bravery carries over to his full credit as Boswell goes on to tell of his "Give us no more of this" and of his expressing himself "in a way that alarmed and distressed me." When the peremptory "Don't let us meet to-morrow" comes, we feel not that Johnson has been blamably irritable but only that we have seen a nature, like ours but much grander, unintentionally provoked beyond endurance. Boswell, of course, had at the moment been himself made "extremely uneasy." "All the harsh observations which I had ever heard made upon his character, crowded into my mind." But in retrospect the causes of this uneasiness had faded away, irrelevant to the grand epiphany to which he had been witness, and we ourselves actively perceive only the universality and not the contingency of the occasion.

But Boswell can preserve not merely the grand essential moments but also the very small ones. It is sometimes said that he does not show us the light, trifling Johnson we know from Burney and Thrale, but consider the following vignette:

Johnson was prevailed with to come sometimes into these [blue-stocking] circles, and did not think himself too grave even for the lively Miss Monckton (now Countess of Corke), who used to have the finest *bit of blue* at the house of her mother, Lady Galway. Her vivacity enchanted the Sage, and they used to talk together with all imaginable ease. A singular instance happened one evening, when she insisted that some of Sterne's writings were very pathetick. Johnson bluntly denied it. "I am sure (said she) they have affected *me*."— "Why, (said Johnson, smiling, and rolling himself about,) that is, because, dearest, you're a dunce." When she some time afterwards mentioned this to him, he said with equal truth and politeness; "Madam, if I had thought so, I certainly should not have said it." [20]

Boswell's quick definition of the established mutual regard of the two, the brief glimpse we get of Johnson's usually ominous tendency to roughness ("bluntly denied") joined to the surprising adroitness and sophistication of his immediate and ultimate responses to Miss Monckton's momentary and fetching vulnerability conspire to make the little scene extremely pleasing. Even so, however, the immediate response would not have given much pleasure if Boswell had not marked Johnson's inner spirit so accurately by his description of the Doctor's physical posture. The language ("dearest") and the movements together wonderfully communicate the delighted premeditation and benign condescension with which the ponderous Johnson makes his affectionate thrust. And so Boswell reveals another aspect, surprising but entirely consonant, of Johnson's astonishing being.

Despite his intention of evoking consistent admiration and reverence for Johnson, Boswell as we have already seen does not suppress our sense of his faults. Boswell set out to write "not his panegyric, which must be all praise, but his Life; which, great and good as he was, must not be supposed to be entirely perfect." [21] Boswell did not suppress faults but deliberately included them and thereby induced Fanny Burney's fear, already noticed, that the portrait of Johnson with all his blemishes would lessen him forever in the eyes of posterity. But Boswell knew that without the blemishes the portrait would not be true and concretely convincing. Unless the reader were to see an image which in its basic structure corresponded to his own imperfect nature, he would not recognize either the paradigmatic likeness or the particular otherness that are the essence of biographical portraiture; he would not admire because he would not believe.[22] Besides, to be as Johnson was, with all his defects, constituted, as Boswell says, "panegyric enough to any man in this state of nature." But Boswell had an artistic motive even higher than verisimilitude for his honesty. He can make Johnson even more admirable by showing that he was so in *spite* of his faults and uglinesses. As in all art, the greater the ugliness overcome, the greater the ultimate beauty and pleasure. As Hume showed long ago,[23] any emotion arising from the contemplation of a painful object is, in the presence of a predominant sentiment of beauty, converted into the higher feeling. Any emotive reaction to faults or ugliness is overcome consistently in Boswell by the emotion attaching to our immediate or residual impression of Johnson's essential greatness and goodness.[24] When Mrs. Piozzi tells us that Johnson was a "gross feeder," the brief image is ugly and painful, while a much more particular and materially ugly description of Johnson's eating by Boswell is not.[25] Mrs. Piozzi's description images her own disgust, Boswell's a more complex but affirmative reaction which assimilates our perception of the intense passion with which Johnson eats to our sense of the gigantic will which drives his being and which does not, except in indifferent matters, break through his moral control. Consistently in the *Life*, as in most of the episodes we have examined, faults are pleasurably rendered as temporary foibles or necessary defects of the great virtues, while the fully represented physical grotesqueness, the eccentricity and ugliness, ultimately serve only to make Johnson's achievement the more concretely real, particular and astonishing.

But even when Johnson's defects cannot be converted to immediately sympathetic pleasure, Boswell faces them directly, in order to show, we may say, how much Johnson can spare. He makes little defense, for instance, of *Taxation No Tyranny*. Johnson should not have written it, and Boswell quotes with approval two animadversions on the pamphlet. Both of these, however, share with Boswell the assumption that the work is an uncharacteristic and unworthy product of the great mind which produced it, and when Boswell goes on to indicate as fully and concretely as he can that Johnson probably shared this view, the effect is complete. Finally, in extreme cases, where Johnson has been excessively rude or violent, Boswell will report an outburst in general terms sufficient to make us understand its character and effect, but not vividly enough to make it actively disagreeable. The most notable example precisely because it is so seldom noted is the occasion when Johnson attacks Boswell himself so fiercely that Boswell is angry for days and almost goes away to Scotland without seeing the Doctor again.[26] The shock was obviously nearly traumatic to Boswell, and affected him personally more deeply perhaps than all but a few of the scenes in the *Life*. His handling of it is characteristic: he *tells* us accurately the substance and effect of Johnson's rudeness, but he does not *show* it to us; in the sequel, however, he dramatizes the reconciliation with great particularity and happy effect. Despite his personal investment, he proportions the weight he gives the scene strictly to its relative value as a sign of his subject—Johnson's character as it is of interest to all men, not Johnson's character as it might appear momentarily to and affect one man. Boswell sees not for himself but for all of us; his book is by no means "one man's recollections of another."

This brings us to our final topic in the *Life:* the general matter of its truth. Most students have emphasized that the strictest truth is essential to biography, but they have meant by truth, ordinarily, authenticity—fidelity to ascertainable empirical fact. The authenticity of Boswell's account has often been investigated and checked against his own records and the records of others. The verdict is nearly unanimous: the *Life* is as authentic as human effort could have made it. Yet we have seen fully characteristic instances when Boswell goes quite beyond the limits of literal truth, as when he dramatizes scenes he has not witnessed, or directly enters Johnson's mind; even the speeches, we have noticed, must be understood as true more in effect than in substance. If, as Johnson himself and many since have insisted, the inherent value of biog-

raphy depends directly upon its literal truth, how can
we justify Boswell's editing, shaping, and evaluation?
More generally, how can we explain the fact that we
experience the full value of Boswell's book while reading
it in complete innocence of all the existing external corroboration of its accuracy? The answer is implicit and to
a degree explicit in all that I have been saying. Certified
truth in Boswell's book is a requisite as in all factual
narrative, but its truth is ultimately relevant not to the
external facts of Johnson's life but to the essence of his
character; for the book is not about an eighteenth-century
man of letters, not about an external life and career, but
about a man, significant independent of history, who
manifested himself in the events of a life and career.
All of Boswell's authenticating assiduity, all the innumerable certified details, are valuable finally not as
they give us true external facts but as evidence of the
conjunction of that magnificent image with reality; like
Defoe's circumstantiality, Boswell's constantly implies that
the fact is not fiction but real; but unlike Defoe's, Boswell's circumstantiality is not a lie. An inherent part of
the pleasure of the character is that it *was* real, and without Boswell's endless certification of what might seem the
aesthetically indifferent reality around it, our pleasure
in the image could not be as certain and full. Our emotion
is toward a timeless image but it is nonetheless an image
of fact with location in time and place. Nevertheless the
only inherently essential fact of the work is the character;
and the truth of the character itself, as we understand by
now, is something internal to the *Life* itself. We know
intuitively that the character is what it appears to be
because it is so complex, so various and astonishing in

its endless manifestations and yet so obviously consistent and coherent as a whole that its image could have proceeded from no cause except itself. It is not, as some have sneeringly said, that we know that Boswell could not have invented Johnson; rather we know with the fullest intuitive certainty that no one—not Defoe, not even Shakespeare—could have invented him. No fictional personality approaches the capacities and complexities of Johnson's. Insofar as the reality of the character is concerned, the book is more compelling than any other evidence of any kind could possibly be. The truth about Johnson's life will change and grow, but the essential truth of his character will never be different from what we feel it to be in Boswell; our residual impression of Johnson must always be such as to produce admiration and reverence. And so we end where we began. Boswell's book is literature because it lifts an aspect of human reality from the contingency of history and displays it as a concrete universal—self-validating, self-intelligible, inherently moving, permanently valuable.

For what we experience finally in the book—and this is the most fundamental source of its literary greatness— is not the sum of Johnson's particular actions but the essence of his character, an essence deeply relevant not to the contingency of history but to the permanence of human nature and therefore immediately to ourselves.

Every man desires to be both bound and free. He desires to be free to express his own deepest passions, and he desires to be bound by the ties of morality and convention that link him to other men in love and respect. It follows from this that he desires at the same time to bind his deepest passions and to break through the internalized restraints of society. His pride requires that he be potent; his dignity requires that he be moral. The powers of most men are unequal to the paradox: dignity suffers when the passionate self breaks down, or corrupts, the moral commitment; or pride is diminished as the self in meeting the commitment succumbs to the seductions of the protean forms of hypocrisy. Literature in general may be understood as, at bottom, a series of symbolic solutions to this paradox, with success dependent upon the degree to which both its dimensions are satisfied. And Johnson's image is the functional core of a great work of literature because his extraordinarily passionate and powerful being, while fully committed to the restraints of convention, morality, and reason, was yet neither corrupted nor rendered impotent. Perpetually he broke powerfully through the ordinary restraints of convention to express his most primal impulses in vindication of his commitment to convention, morality and reason. He thereby created his dignity and justified his pride on the most general human grounds, so that his image could become for all of us a token of the simultaneous freedom and commitment which is possible to human beings. Symbolically in our imaginative sympathy and actually as an example, that image frees us from the burdens of conventional impotence and falsity—from the rehearsed response, the coward's stance, the liar's quinsy—and restores our dignity, and our pride in ourselves and in the human nature which we share with him. That is why the pleasure of the book is so real and so deep.

Johnson's image is therefore one of the most valuable of our cultural possessions, but without Boswell it would never have been freed from the bondage of time. His book is, as Carlyle said, "a revocation of the edict of Destiny; so that Time shall not utterly, not so soon by several centuries, have dominion over us.[27] Not over Johnson, notice, but over us—who have our stake in Johnson. Boswell's construction of his book was a supremely important artistic act. Because it was so fully artistic, however, it *is* fully real and therefore has seemed to many to manifest no art at all. But it should be clear from what we have said that the *Life of Samuel Johnson* is a great book not because the subject was great or because the biographer was great but because both were great; it was a magnificent literary symbiosis. Johnson was all activity, Boswell all potentiality. He—a truly reverent man, as Carlyle says—filled himself with Johnson's greatness and displayed it to posterity shorn of accident and unblemished by any stain of his own private feeling or immense personal ego. That ego indeed had been deeply wounded in the midst of his task when he learned what Johnson had said of him in his letters to Mrs. Thrale, but this did not at all deflect him from his high purpose.

Johnson, if he had known, would have been more grateful to Boswell than posterity has often been. "Sir, it was generous and noble beyond expectation." But even in his life he was not indifferent to Boswell's devotion. We remember the unusual gesture he made in going with Boswell down to Harwich to see him off to Holland. One of the finest moments in the *Life* is our view of him tarrying on the Harwich pier as the receding Boswell perceives him in the distance, "rolling his majestic frame." [28] The moment is strangely moving, because it triggers in proportion to its slightness such a flood of sentiment. Boswell's two epithets render the for once in-articulate figure a sudden and forceful evocation of all the benevolent affection that our experience as shaped by Boswell has attached to his image. Boswell repaid the Doctor for his kindness. His majestic frame will roll there forever in its particular and universal humanity.

A brief postscript about the relevance of the conception offered here of the form of Boswell's *Johnson* to the general problem of literary form in all factual narratives. We may say first that to the degree that any factual narrative is responded to as literature, its form may be analyzed as inherently the cause of an effect. And insofar as the form has the capacity to produce an effect, it will have raised human fact out of contingency and made it concretely present as a striking but inherently probable manifestation of complete and morally determinate human thought, character, or action, individual or collective.

It is this non-contingent, universal quality of narratives like Boswell's and Gibbon's which accounts for the indubitable fact that they remain of timeless value while works dealing with contingent aspects of the same subjects are perpetually superseded and absorbed in new expressions. Both kinds of history depend upon truth, but in different ways. The effect of Gibbon's work, for instance, depends on a very simple and unchanging truth which in no way either limits or is limited by more complex explanatory truths about Rome's fall. The effect depends on the undeniable fact that Rome can be viewed by all human beings as a true high civilization, that it passed out of existence, and that none of the actors in the fall could fully comprehend or in any way prevent it. The fall was striking and necessary and therefore, when presented as Gibbon concretely presents it, inherently moving.

In the highest factual literature, therefore, the conditions of literary success approach those of fictional literature, but we must not therefore confuse the two modes. In fiction, the form must totally subsume the whole matter of the work. In most factual works, even when there is literary intent, a good deal of material must necessarily remain only passively adjusted to the form. When effect in factual works is produced in spite of, rather than through, the facts, as in Strachey's sketch of Dr. Colbatch, the result is brilliant but cheap. Factual literature is inescapably connected with external reality, and in the best factual works a necessary part of our pleasure, as we have seen, comes from feeling that, in Carlyle's phrase, the events related "did in very deed occur." [29] Thus, though the formula is the same, the criterion of imaginative commitment in fiction and fact is different; fact *is* stranger than fiction, and when fact is rendered universally true, it can and ought to claim a benefit from its strangeness and particularity that fiction cannot. But the realms of fiction and fact, so absolutely distinct at their extremities of pure imagination and pure explanation, nevertheless come very close to one another at the point where Shakespeare's history plays, say, and *Paradise Lost* on the one hand—fully concrete but dependent on a presumptive relation to fact—look toward works like *The Prelude* and Boswell's *Johnson* on the other which, though largely concrete, demand acceptance as true fact. And even at the extremes, pure explanation, as in Hume's "On Tragedy," can give concrete pleasure in proportion to its clarity, coherence, concision and native significance, while even the veriest work of the imagination must ultimately be dependent on the facts of human nature and existence. (Johnson himself made the point clearly: "The value of every story depends on its being true. A story is a picture either of an individual or of human nature in general: if it be false, it is a picture of nothing.") [30]

But our present concern is with those works which, clearly factual, are nonetheless clearly literature. We can see now why there are so few such works. Fact is seldom such as to be even the potential cause of universal effects. If the decline of the Roman Empire had not been an inherently grand spectacle, Gibbon could never have made it so and given us the gravely sublime pleasure of perceiv- ing the internal human causes of its inevitable fall. If seventeenth-century England had not really produced a nineteenth-century England that was in some perspectives inherently superior to it, while retaining its heritage and essential values, Macaulay could never have shown us the spectacle that causes the grand pride he makes us feel.[31] And even when the facts are potentially productive of art, the man and the occasion rarely meet. The fully imaginative artist has subjects at any time, but the decline of the Roman Empire was available as literature only to the unique gifts of a man who had inherited the special values and attitudes of a single time and place. So it is also with Macaulay, to say nothing of the miraculous conjunction of Johnson and Boswell, a special providence for which humanity must ever be grateful.

The very great barriers to full literary success in factual narrative are illustrated by Truman Capote's *In Cold Blood*. Here an artist of great capacity seized the ac- cidentally available opportunity and realized it to the full extent of its potentialities. Displaying powers of

imaginative reconstruction and synthesis equalled only by
Boswell, he yet failed, I believe, to achieve the highest
kind of factual literature. Capote does an extraordinary
thing. He makes us appreciate the full horror and senseless
cruelty of the inexplicable, bloody, night-time murder of
a whole family remarkable for its normal decency in a
broad social context of normal, uneventful decency, but
he makes us feel at the same time a much more unusual
thing. He makes us feel for the murderers not anger or a
desire for vengeance but rather a peculiar if limited
sympathy. The sympathy can be defined by saying that
we see Dick's and Perry's actions as the result of their
whole nature and lives, for which they are not to blame,
and that consequently we do not hate them or desire
their deaths; but neither, on the other hand, do we feel
toward them any real mercy or forgiveness. This effect is
the strength but also the limitation of the book. Our
failure to feel mercy and forgiveness means that finally
we do not recognize Dick and Perry as fully sharing our
common nature; we feel that we could not, in any con-
ceivable circumstances, have done what they did. Our
intimate knowledge of the murderers widens our view of
human existence but it does not make us better able to
bear it. The same is true from the point of view of the
victims. When Hamlet dies, or when Rome falls, we
perceive how human beings are involved in their own
necessary destruction, but we feel strongly after the fact
that even in the face of destruction it was worthwhile to
be Hamlet, worthwhile that Rome was. But the Clutters'
death, we are made to see, is a monstrous accident with
no moral relevance whatever to them. There is no ethical
consonance in it, so that we do not feel retrospectively
that it was worthwhile for them to have lived, or that to

have lived and died as they did would be worthwhile to us. The whole story offers only a limited catharsis and no residual grandeur. The defect is not in Capote's art, except as it selected the subject, but in the subject itself, inherently defective because not sufficiently universal.

History and biography then cannot often aspire to the purity of Boswell or Gibbon. Indeed, to seek after concreteness and effect would often prevent them from fulfilling their usual purpose—true knowledge and understanding of the contingent past. Modern history, for that matter, is not often guilty of trying to be literature. The high level of general culture among a small elite class which was the great achievement of eighteenth- and nineteenth-century civilization permitted and encouraged the historian or biographer to aim at both historical truth and literary force; the concerns of the scholar were not separate from the concerns of the human being. Now, of course, we have the often-lamented gap between the scholar and the journalist, between inert truth and cheap effect. The journalist, however, now seems pushed by the rising level of general culture towards adequacy to the human truth, and the scholar by the same phenomenon encouraged to discover that, though fact needs to be true to be valuable, it need not be dead in order to be true. Capote's book, Schlesinger's *Thousand Days*, Schorer's *Lewis* and Ellmann's *Joyce*, together with others that have recently appeared, may thus be harbingers of a renaissance in factual literature. We may hope so, for as Herbert Muller has shown, by precept and example, the past, of which materially we have recovered so much, must sometimes be put to immediately human uses if it is to serve us as fully as it may.

The Uses of Autobiography in the Eighteenth Century

DONALD GREENE / *University of Wisconsin*

The best biography of Samuel Johnson is not Boswell's. In spite of Macaulay's magisterial pronouncement —which sounds rather more like a sudden journalistic brain-wave than a piece of considered criticism—that Boswell is as decidedly the first of biographers as Homer is the first of epic poets and Shakespeare the first of dramatists, there exists an account of Johnson's life which has always impressed me as far more vivid, authentic, and memorable than any part of Boswell's, excellent as Boswell's may be in its own way. I should like to present an extract from it. Professor Clifford, Johnson's distinguished modern biographer, displayed what has always seemed to me excellent judgment in beginning his own biography, *Young Sam Johnson,* with a quotation, not from anything in Boswell, but from this:

September 7, 1709, I was born at Lichfield, My mother had a very difficult and dangerous labour, and was assisted by George Hector, a man-midwife of great reputation. I was born almost dead and could not cry for some time. When he had me in his arms, he said, "Here is a brave boy." . . . My Father being that year Sheriff of Lichfield, and to ride the circuit of the County next day, which was a ceremony then performed with great pomp, he was asked by my mother, "Whom he would invite to the Riding?" and answered, "All the town now."

And a little later,

This year, in Lent [17]12, I was taken to London, to be touched for the evil by Quen Anne. My mother was at Nicholson's, the famous bookseller, in Little Britain. My mother, then with child, concealed her pregnancy, that she might not be hindered from the journey. I always retained some memory of this journey, though I was then but thirty months old. I remembered a little dark room behind the kitchen, where the jack-weight fell through a hole in the floor, into which I once slipped my leg. I seem to remember that I played with a string and a bell, which my cousin Isaac Johnson gave me; that there was a cat with a white collar, and a dog called Chops that leaped over a stick. . . . [My mother] bought me a small silver cup and spoon, marked SAM. I. lest if they had been marked S.I., which was her name, they should, upon her death, have been taken from me. She bought me a speckled linen frock, which I knew afterwards by the name of my London frock. The cup was one of the last pieces of plate which dear Tetty sold in our distress. She bought at the same time two teaspoons, and till my manhood she had no more.[1]

You will have recognized the author—Samuel Johnson himself, writing at the age of fifty-five, famous and at last financially secure; writing during one of his periods of most severe mental depression; writing, Professor Clifford suggests, to help preserve his sanity ("These little memorials sooth my mind," he comments, after noting down one of the apparently rare bits of praise that his mother bestowed on him when he was a boy); writing perhaps in the spirit of what we now call psychoanalysis, in which we attempt to relive our early lives again and in the process somehow manage to exorcize some of our psychic traumas and enable ourselves to go on living and working with greater equanimity—much as Wordsworth does in *The Prelude*.

What do we get in this piece of autobiography—unfortunately only a small surviving fragment—that we do not get in Boswell? A number of fairly important things, I think. For one, we get authentic reports of subjective states, as contrasted with the often merely conjectural ones found in Boswell—conjectures which sometimes seem inept and potentially misleading. For instance, when he and Johnson are travelling by coach to Oxford, Boswell tells us, "He bore the journey very well, and seemed to feel himself elevated as he approached Oxford, that magnificent and venerable seat of Learning, Orthodoxy, and Toryism." [2] What evidence Boswell had for this diagnosis of Johnson's emotional condition, he does not tell us; and we may well question whether Johnson's good spirits at this point, if they existed at all, were completely the effect of contemplating the philosophical notion of Oxford University. They may at least in part have been due simply to relief at nearing the end of a tedious journey, or the prospective pleasure of meeting old friends, or even that of a good supper—he was probably hungry, since at dinner on the road he had immortalized the mutton served him by declaring it "ill-fed, ill-killed, ill-kept, and ill-drest." One may even speculate that a partial cause of the elevation was the prospect of escaping at last from Boswell's chattering at his side, which he had patiently endured for several hours. I have little doubt that many of the stereotypes we have of Johnson's arrogance, his fanatical devotion to reactionary Toryism, and other important matters owe a good deal to

Boswell's conjectures about his motives, conjectures which are often due to Boswell's foisting his own emotional patterns on to Johnson. This sort of thing is of course a constant danger for the biographer, whose motto, when it comes to analyzing the motivation of his subject, probably ought *not* to be "Look into thy heart and write." In the autobiographical fragment, however, when Johnson writes of the recollection of his mother's praise, "These little memorials soothe my mind," we have no reason to doubt it. When he writes of the cup "which *dear* Tetty sold in our distress," we have a piece of incontestably authentic evidence about one element at least of Johnson's feelings toward his wife, as well as about the emotional impact which poverty made on him—it is revealing that in the 1760's, freed from financial worry for the rest of his life, he still casts his eye backward a decade or more to the times of "our distress."

Another thing we get in the autobiographical fragment that we do not in Boswell is a far greater concentration of what Johnson in his great essay on biography in *Rambler* 60 called the "invisible circumstances which . . . are more important than public occurrences," those "domestic privacies . . . the minute details of daily life, where exterior appendages are cast aside," which in Johnson's view are the heart of good biography. Certainly we get such details in Boswell, who was an apt pupil of his master here: we get the details which seem to have made such an impression on Macaulay and other readers—the rolling gait, the singed wig, the twitchings and mutterings, the compulsive mannerisms, the less than dainty table-manners. But of these, amusing as they are at one's first reading of Boswell we may perhaps remark what Johnson goes on in his essay to remark about the methods of run-of-the-mill biographers, "If now and then they condescend to inform the world of particular facts, they are not always so happy as to select the most important." As an illustration of such unimportant detail, Johnson mentions "the only circumstance by which Tickell has distinguished Addison from the rest of mankind, 'the irregularity of his pulse.' " As an example of *significant* detail, on the other hand, he cites Sallust, "the great master of nature," as he calls him, who notes that Catiline's "walk was now quick, and again slow," as an indication, Johnson says, of a mind revolving something with violent commotion.[3] How rich in significant detail Johnson's autobiographical account is! We get a far more vivid and concrete picture of Michael Johnson from the reminiscence of his pride at his son's birth—"All the town now!"—than from several dry and often dangerously speculative pages about him in Hawkins and Boswell. How much we learn about Sarah Johnson from the story of her concealment of her pregnancy in order to bring her son to London to be touched for the Evil—obviously that son inherited much of his determination from her! And how much we learn about the son's feelings toward his parents from the very fact that he remembers these things about them and thinks them worth recording!

Surely such an "invisible circumstance" as Michael Johnson's exultation over the boy's birth is "more important" to us in the business of constructing an authentic picture of Samuel's childhood background than the extremely dubious conjecture put forward by Hawkins and repeated by Boswell that Michael's political leanings were Jacobite, in spite of the imposing edifice of further conjecture about Samuel's political opinions that has been

erected by later students on this flimsy foundation. From
the little story of "All the town now" we learn that Michael
was ambitious, that he was capable of exuberance, that he
was immensely proud of the existence of the son born to
him so late in life—all of them facts which contribute a
good deal to our understanding of that son's psychological
make-up. An extremely industrious and lucky later biographer *might* have encountered this piece of information
recorded in the reminiscences of old Lichfield neighbors
of the Johnsons, though he would have had a hard task
arriving at an accurate determination of its authenticity,
mixed in, as it would undoubtedly have been, with much
apocryphal legend. The fact is however that neither
Hawkins, nor Boswell—even with the assistance of the
admirable Edmund Hector—nor even the indefatigable
Aleyn Lyell Reade did recover it, or anything equally illuminating about the intimate circumstances of Johnson's
early family life from non-Johnsonian sources. Indeed, one
feels like asserting that the few scraps that have survived
from Johnson's autobiography have thrown more light on
the first fifteen or so years of Johnson's life than all the
efforts of his later biographers combined; though from that
roster we must omit Reade and Professor Clifford himself.
The point is of course that the autobiographer has complete access, and the biographer has generally very little, to
these "invisible circumstances" which, as Johnson assures
us and as I imagine all of us here agree, are more important
than the "public occurrences" of a man's life.

Another matter: it may be conceded that the knowledge
of Michael Johnson's elation and of Sarah Johnson's concealment of her pregnancy and her marking the silver cup
with "Sam. I." instead of "S.I." and of Johnson and his

wife having once been in such a state of financial distress that they were reduced to selling the souvenir cup contributes significantly to our understanding of important aspects of Johnson's life and personality. But what are we to make of the cat with a white collar and the dog named Chops that leaped over a stick and the little dark room behind the kitchen where the jack-weight fell through a hole in the floor into which little Sam's leg slipped? If the biographer were to uncover such facts—if, for instance, a floor-plan of Nicholson's house in Little Britain had survived, or if, improbably, dog-licenses had been required at the time and an industrious researcher had sifted the parish records and learned of the existence of Chops—what use could he possibly make of them? None at all, I think; when he came to write up his notes, those that bore the information about Chops and the hole for the jack-weight would surely be relegated to the heap of discards. One can imagine the amused contempt which reviewers, especially British reviewers, would express at the misguided industry of the American scholar who had thought the name of a dog at the house where Johnson spent a few days in 1712 worth recording.[4] And yet Johnson, writing at the age of fifty-five, thought it worth recording.

The point, of course, and Johnson well knew that this was the point, is that the significance of Chops is not Chops himself but the fact that Chops impinged on young Sam's consciousness. He is significant in the same way that little Stephen Dedalus's moo-cow and his aunt's two velvet-backed brushes (in *Portrait of the Artist as a Young Man*) are significant and worth recording. Johnson knew as well as Joyce that the inner life of the individual is made up of such states of consciousness in which one is aware of

certain phenomena and not others, and that a valid account
of that inner life must record them.[5] Later writers and
psychologists, of course, came to recognize that fact; Wordsworth and Joyce were to insist, rightly, on the importance
of these puzzling, yet vastly important, memories, these
"epiphanies" as Joyce called them. Freud as we know
erected a whole imposing science of psychoanalysis on the
basis of such "free association." We can perhaps imagine
what a psychoanalytic biographer might make of the little
dark room with the mysterious, frightening hole, into
which the young boy's leg slipped—it could conceivably be
expanded into an elaborate theory of early trauma about
sex that accounts for Johnson's marrying a woman twenty-
four years older than he. In spite of the possibility of such
extravagance, however, few of us would deny that memories of this kind, however interpreted, do constitute an
important part of one's psychic life; and Johnson's recognition that they should be recorded and studied is remark-
ably perceptive and advanced—though nowadays students
of Johnson should not be too surprised at being told of his
precocity as a psychologist. Of course Freudian (and Joy-
cean and Wordsworthian) theory derives in the end from
Locke's psychology of association, with which Johnson was
perfectly familiar and which he fully accepted. The point
to be made here is that *only* the subject has full access to
this material; it can be made public only by some form of
autobiography, oral or written. The biographer who attempts a psychoanalytic biography without such material
provided by the subject is as handicapped as a psychiatrist
with notebook in hand sitting in frustration at the head of
a vacant couch would be. Without such data, the analyst
would either have to abandon his project or else resort to

making up his own "data," "reconstructing" it from biography—a procedure no reputable analyst would condone for a moment, even though such travesties of analytic method have been perpetrated on historic figures: on Johnson himself, recently on Whittaker Chambers, and even, apparently with the assistance of Freud himself, on Woodrow Wilson.[6]

The fourth and final thing I want to suggest that autobiography furnishes which is not furnished by biography is the revelation of the writer's personality provided by the *tone* of the autobiographical text, by the emotional overtones conveyed in the prose style employed by the writer of his own life. (Autobiographies are usually in prose, though not always—Hobbes's is in Latin verse; and certainly the verse form of such autobiographical works as "Verses on the Death of Doctor Swift" and the "Epistle to Arbuthnot" contributes substantially to the pictures of Swift and Pope left in the reader's mind.) This is not to say that the tone is always to be taken, so to speak, at its face value. William Hickey's autobiography, which was republished a few years ago, apparently with the hope of making it into a best-seller—it was advertised as being as juicy as Boswell's journals—is composed in dashing, devil-may-care prose, intended to impress the reader with the subject's indefatigable rakishness and insouciance.[7] A few pages of this kind of thing go a long way; Hickey continues relentlessly for several hundred and soon succeeds in boring the reader and raising the inevitable deflating question, "What is the poor man compensating for, anyway?" Still, that Hickey should have chosen to adopt and cling to this tone is itself a useful piece of evidence for a diagnosis of Hickey, if Hickey were an interesting enough fellow for us to want to make the effort. The bare, unadorned, economical style of Johnson's own autobiographical fragment—a beautiful style in itself, which must surprise readers familiar only with Johnson's *Rambler* style —immediately raises the question of why he should have adopted it here, when there were so many other styles and tones available to him. It tells us something about Johnson, conceivably something important; just what that something is, the student may decide for himself, but in itself it adds another piece of authentic data to those from which a valid picture of Johnson may be constructed.

The external biographer's style on the other hand tends to obscure and even distort the picture of the subject, especially when the biographer has a high opinion of his own importance in relation to his subject. It might be argued that, just as *Lycidas* tells us very little about its nominal subject, Edward King, but a great deal about young John Milton, and Lytton Strachey's *Queen Victoria* less about the Queen than about Strachey and his generation, so from Boswell's *Life of Johnson* we emerge with a much fuller and more vivid picture of James Boswell than we do of Samuel Johnson—and why not, since so much of the work derives from that enormous autobiographical monument, Boswell's *Journals?* Even when records of the subject in his own writing are embedded in such biography, the context may tend to distort them. An extract from Victoria's journals or letters surrounded by Strachey's acid commentary gives a very different effect from the same extract read in isolation, or in the context of the journal or the letters as a whole. For myself, I much prefer to read Johnson's letters in R. W. Chapman's fine edition than scattered through Boswell; their effect there is quite different; Johnson comes through much more vividly in such isolation than in sporadic gleams through the surrounding Boswellian fog.

You will have gathered by this time that what I am trying to do here is to enter a plea for greater attention to be paid to autobiography, especially eighteenth-century British autobiography, than literary students have been in the habit of giving. Biography itself, goodness knows, is a neglected *genre*. But no good will result, I think, from limiting the definition of biography so as to exclude autobiography. On the contrary, it seems to me that the health and welfare of the study of biography will be enhanced, not endangered, by the inclusion in it of a consideration of its generally outcast stepsister. Indeed, when one begins to examine the basic problems of biography, it proves difficult arbitrarily to eliminate autobiography from the discussion. After all, the final product of both, the lasting work of art, is the account of the life of some human being; who set that account down on paper is more or less irrelevant, except from the point of view of someone who himself plans at some time or other to write a biography—or perhaps an autobiography. Not all of us here plan to do so; but all of us, as students of literature, do have an interest in the completed work as a specimen of literature.

In support of my plea that more serious attention be paid to autobiography, I again wish to cite Samuel Johnson. Johnson was, we know, the pioneer theorist as well as a pioneer practitioner of biography; his *Rambler* No. 60, published in October 1750, a very great piece of criticism, sets out the basic desiderata of biography, considered as literature. Johnson here is not concerned with biography

as a branch of history, as merely a record of events which
have taken place in the past. Indeed, Johnson's attitude
toward history is hardly the usual one; his point of view
seems to be that, after all, innumerable events have taken
place in the past, far too many to be recorded or compre-
hended by a single mind; the mere indiscriminate recording of them, in an indistinguishable jumble, is unfeasible
and pointless. There must therefore always be selection,
and Johnson has grave doubts that the events conventionally selected by historians to be recorded, those "perform-
ances and incidents which produce vulgar greatness," are
likely to be the most valuable; as a moralist, he has no
great faith in the set of values by which the average man—
or the average historian or reader of history—sorts out the
events of the past for recording. "Histories of the downfall
of kingdoms, and revolutions of empires," he writes, "are
read with great tranquillity: the imperial tragedy pleases
common auditors only by its pomp of ornament and
grandeur of ideas." And if the result of reading history is
only emotional tranquillity or, at best, superficial stimu-
lation, if our deeper feelings and real values are not affected by it, then we are, of course, doomed to repeat it.
Hence biography is potentially more valuable than conventional history—biography, which achieves, or should
achieve, its effect on the reader by bringing about "an act
of the imagination" on his part, in which he empathizes,
identifies, with the subject of the biography—re-enacts as
it were the life of that individual, extends his own moral
horizons by vicarious experience. It may perhaps be of
some comfort to us here to note that the better historians
of the past two centuries have also done much soul-
searching about just what the function of historiography

is and how it can best be fulfilled, though without arriving at any generally agreed on answer. The most striking development in recent British historiography has, of course, been the revolution effected by Sir Lewis Namier and his followers, in which biography has virtually supplanted the study of those mysterious entities "movements," "trends," even "ideologies"; under its influence, British political history has come recently to be written less in terms of hypothetical "isms" and more in terms of what individual participants in the events of the time thought, felt, and did.[8] As so often, Johnson again seems conspicuously ahead of his own time: throughout the nineteenth century, biography, as Strachey complained, continued to pursue the old Plutarchan ideal of suppressing uncomfortable and too revealing facts about the subject in order to set "good examples" before the eyes of its readers, forgetting that, as Johnson would have heartily agreed, "human beings are too important to be treated as mere symptoms of the past." [9]

All of us are, or should be, familiar with *Rambler* 60 and Johnson's great apologia for biography. We too often forget, however, that he supplemented it with an equally powerful apologia for *auto*biography, as the most useful, and therefore the highest, form of biography. This is of course *Idler* 84, written nine years later. In it he begins by considering the claims to attention of the novel (or rather the romance) and of history, stressing their limitations ("Between falsehood and useless truth there is little difference," he says of history). He places general biography higher than either—"those relations which are levelled with the general surface of life, which tell not how any man became great, but how he was made happy; not how he lost the favour of his prince but how he became discontented with himself." He continues,

Those relations are therefore commonly of most value in which the writer tells his own story. He that recounts the life of another commonly dwells most upon conspicuous events, lessens the familiarity of his tale to increase its dignity, shows his favorite at a distance decorated and magnified . . . and endeavours to hide the man that he may produce a hero.

"The writer of his own life," Johnson points out, "has at least the first qualification of an historian, the knowledge of the truth"; and then he proceeds to deal with the usual charge against autobiography, that its writer has more motive than the allegedly impartial biographer for *suppressio veri* and *assertio falsi*. Not at all, says Johnson: many motives for distortion enter into the mind of the biographer which will not afflict that of the autobiographer—"The zeal of gratitude, the ardour of patriotism, fondness for an opinion, or fidelity to a party may easily overpower the vigilance of a mind habitually well disposed, and prevail over unassisted and unfriended veracity." One wonders how many of these motives Johnson might have detected in Boswell's *Life* if he had been able to see it—he did, we know, see parts of Boswell's journal, from which it was derived, and approved; but it is not hard to find passages in the *Life*, often ones which have been very influential in creating the modern image of Johnson, which have been drastically altered from the text of the journal, presumably as the result of such extraneous motives as fondness for an opinion or fidelity to a party.

"But he that speaks of himself," Johnson concludes, "has no motives to falsehood or partiality but self-love; by which all have so often been betrayed that all are on the watch against its artifices." This vigilance will presumably enable us to put into perspective apologias for one's own actions—as for instance, the memoirs of Sarah Churchill, Duchess of Marlborough, which Johnson reviewed "in depth" when they appeared in 1742. In his review, Johnson considers the objection that, whereas the Duchess had a better opportunity than anyone else to know what went on behind the scenes in Queen Anne's reign, at the same time no one had a greater motive to distort the account of it to her own advantage. If so, the cynic (or Marxist) may ask, "What purpose are such relations, except to produce a general incredulity? The man who knows not the truth cannot, and he that knows it will not, tell it; what then remains but to distrust every relation and live in perpetual negligence of past events; or what is still more disagreeable, in perpetual suspense?" Not so, says Johnson the staunch empiricist: "Distrust is a necessary qualification of the student of history . . . Truth, though not always obvious, *is* generally discoverable, nor," he adds, "is it anywhere more likely to be found than in private memoirs. . . ."

It might also be noted that in the introductory pages to the *Life of Johnson,* where Boswell attempts to formulate his biographical motives and principles, he begins by acknowledging the justice of what Johnson says in *Idler* 84, that every man's life is best written by himself. Since Johnson has not done so, Boswell continues, he will do the next best thing and follow the example of Mason in his life of Gray, by producing, wherever it is in his power, Johnson's "own minutes, letters, or conversation," furnishing "whatever narrative is necessary to explain, connect, and supply" these. Most of us would agree, I think, that this is hardly an accurate description of what in fact the *Life* turns out to be: for all that Johnson's own words are supposed to remain central to it, the work is dominated by Boswell—naturally enough, when so much of it comes from Boswell's journals, which after all were intended to record Boswell's life, not Johnson's. But at least Boswell here pays lip service to Johnson's principle that auto-biography is the best kind of biography. A later example of the biography that remains essentially autobiography, in which that ideal is more successfully realized, I would argue, than in Boswell's is George Otto Trevelyan's fine life of his uncle Lord Macaulay. "His own letters"—and journal entries—"supply the deficiencies of the biog-rapher," says Trevelyan, who wisely lets them speak for themselves, and though linking them with a connecting narrative at least as informative as Boswell's, he does an admirable job of keeping his own personality from intrud-ing and overshadowing that of his subject.

So far my task has been to try to justify the paying of greater attention to autobiography than students of the eighteenth century have generally been in the habit of doing; to justify it on the grounds set out by Johnson, that it is the queen of the various forms of biography, that it is by its nature best able to fulfill the desiderata of biography generally. I should now like to point out what a wealth of autobiographical material there is available to students of the century, material that is of immense value to those who really wish to come to grips with the social, political, intellectual, and literary history of the time, and to enter a plea that more opportunities be provided for our students to make contact with it. Biography as such does occasionally win recognition by way of an occasional course offered in it as a literary *genre;* but usually the only form in which the student, even the student specializing in the eighteenth century, encounters the rich autobiographical material of the period in formal course work is in the form of a few snippets from Gibbon's autobiography or Boswell's journals, from Walpole's or Chesterfield's letters, in an anthology used in an undergraduate survey course. He may then go through many years of further study ostensibly of the eighteenth century encountering such things only by chance. This neglect, it seems to me, is at least partly responsible for the tendency I and others have noticed and deplored in graduate students and younger scholars of the period for the eighteenth century to become little more than a collection of nebulous abstractions, bodiless "isms" of one kind or another—Augustanism, humanism, neo-classicism, and the rest of the dreary catalogue—floating about in a vacuum, acting and interacting with one another, but attached to concrete, living human beings of the century in only the most tenuous way. This is surely a shocking way to treat a period which, whatever else it may be, was crammed with vivid, exuberant, complex human experience—"What should books teach us except how better to enjoy life or to endure it?" as Johnson said. One way that might help to keep it from dissolving into a set of airy abstractions would be to recommend that all graduate students specializing in the period do a substantial course of reading in the autobiographies, diaries, memoirs, and letters of the century.

This collocation of nouns, by the way—letters, diaries, autobiographies, and memoirs—happens to be the heading used by a section of the *Cambridge Bibliography of English Literature* (Volume II, pages 133-140) which is, or could be, of the greatest use to the student of the period. Although for conciseness I have used the word "autobiography" in this title of this chapter, I find it as difficult as the Cambridge bibliographers to make sharp distinctions between the *genres* designated in these various ways. If one is going to put down on paper a first-hand account of what has happened to one, it does not really matter very much what form that record takes; they shade imperceptibly into one another. Swift's *Journal to Stella* consists of memoranda jotted down by Swift at the end of each day, then collected and mailed to Stella at intervals of a week or so. While they remain in Swift's room, I suppose we should call them a diary; when they enter the post, they suddenly become a letter. Johnson's *Journey to the Western Islands of Scotland* is, among other things, an autobiographical memoir of how he spent three interesting months in the year 1773; a great deal of it, however, is a revision of a series of letters he wrote to Mrs. Thrale en route; if he had not mailed these letters, but kept them in a memorandum book and handed the book to Mrs. Thrale on his return to London, I suppose we should call it a journal. And so on. It seems useless to try to distinguish rigidly among these terms.

By way of encouragement, I have prepared a specimen syllabus that might be used for a reading course in eighteenth-century autobiographical literature (see p. 111). It would be foolishly wasteful, I think, to try to present this material in a lecture course: as Johnson remarked two centuries ago, "Lectures were once useful; but now, when all can read and books are so numerous, lectures are unnecessary"—he was as usual ahead of his time; ahead of *our* time, in fact. The main thing is to encourage students to read it; the reading presents few difficulties, and it should suffice for the student to meet the supervisor of the course for a few minutes once a week or even once a fortnight to report on what he has read and raise any questions which may have come up during his reading. (I have to confess that only one of the institutions where I have taught has been enlightened enough to let me offer such a course formally; I do not understand why more graduate schools, or for that matter undergraduate colleges, are reluctant to let supervised reading like this be done for credit.)

The list of suggested readings I give here is of course only a small selection from many that could be listed. Naturally, it includes most of my own favorites, but the teacher can reorder it so that *his* favorites are not neglected. Moreover, the student should be encouraged to browse through bibliographies or along library shelves to find things that seem particularly appealing to him. He undoubtedly will find them, for here is God's plenty. There used to be a cliché, not often heard nowadays but worthy of being revived, to the effect that the eighteenth century was the great age of memoir-, journal-, and letter-writing. William Matthews's bibliography, *British Autobiographies* (Berkeley and Los Angeles, 1955), listing some 300 to 400 titles in the late seventeenth and the eighteenth century, gives some idea of the scope; in addition, his *British Diaries* (Berkeley and Los Angeles, 1950) lists another 700 or 800 titles for the century. The objection may be heard that some of them are after all pretty trivial. Should the student, it will be asked, be encouraged to spend his valuable time reading the day-to-day memoranda of a drowsy country parson like James Woodforde or the reminiscences of a vulgar nonentity like Laetitia Pilkington when he could be reading—what? the latest monograph by a twentieth-century student explaining how the whole of the eighteenth century can be digested by memorizing a handful of neat formulas, "Augustan humanism," perhaps, or "the neo-classic sensibility," and thus tucked into a pigeon-hole and so disposed of permanently? I can only answer, yes, he should be so encouraged.

The title I have given this chapter is "the uses of autobiography." Some of its uses for the modern student I have already hinted. It will anchor him firmly in the concrete reality of the eighteenth century, and help to keep him from being blown about helplessly by the winds of current fashions in abstract theorizing about it. It will do this more effectively, I think, than later biography will, unless, like Trevelyan's *Macaulay,* that biography contains a large portion of the subject's *ipsissima verba* and the biographer is self-effacing. Otherwise, the subject has already been put at one remove and a barrier been erected between the reader and the subject and the subject's time. It is, or should be, thrilling for the young student, after a long course of people and books telling him how the eighteenth-century mind worked, to be able to turn to the eighteenth century's own words and say to himself, "Here, at last, is the way it was." Such a course of reading as I have suggested will also introduce him to a good deal of literature that is very fine, merely in itself: Hervey's, Gibbon's, Lady Mary's, Walpole's, Hume's memoir-, letter-, and journal-writing are English prose of the highest order. Contemporary autobiographical writing is also one of the finest sources of concrete historical knowledge available to the student; and most of the ills of eighteenth-century literary scholarship today—as I have hinted, it is by no means free from ills—stem, I think, from ignorance of history, or rather the currency of much demonstrably false history. The *CBEL* places its list of "Letters, Diaries, Autobiographies, and Memoirs" of the time under the heading "Social History." But they reveal much more than merely social history. John Carswell and L. A. Dralle justify their excellent edition of Bubb Dodington's diary, the first since its original publication, in mangled form, in 1784, on the ground that "it can now be seen as one of the cardinal documents of eighteenth-century politics." [10] Political historians are more and more returning to such contemporary, first-hand records by the participants in the political events of the time for authentic evidence of what actually went on, and to correct the misconceptions generated by reliance by students on structures of erroneous speculation erected by later writers of monographs, each building on the foundations of conjecture laid by his predecessors. Historians of ideas in the eighteenth century would do well to heed their example.

One false historical notion which I think a thorough acquaintance with the vast autobiographical literature of the eighteenth century will eventually help to destroy is the one so dear to literary historians of a sharp discontinuity between the "sensibility" of the eighteenth century and that of the so-called "Romantic" period—a notion which, after suffering some attrition since its heyday, when it was the gospel of Victorian academics, has recently shown signs of taking on a new lease of life, largely perhaps through the influence of Northrop Frye. In saying this, I am taking issue with the latest of the small handful of treatises that have been written on autobiography as a literary *genre,* John M. Morris's *Versions of the Self* (New York, 1966). Mr. Morris takes, on the one hand, the autobiographies of Roger North and Edward Gibbon, as illustrating what he calls "The Normal Vision" of the eighteenth century, and, on the other, Wordsworth's *Prelude* and John Stuart Mill's autobiography, together with their predecessors, as he regards them, Bunyan, Cowper, and Boswell, as "Agents of the New." The difference between them, we are to believe, is that "The struggle of the soul to find and be itself is one of the great modern enterprises," [11] though its alleged modernity is so hedged about with foreshadowings, especially in the way of religious autobiography—which a glance at Matthews will show to have flourished mightily in the eighteenth century—as to make the thesis fairly tentative even in the context of the monograph itself. This is not the time and place to enter on a detailed critique of the book's methods and assumptions. But perhaps it is appropriate to conclude this chapter by at least raising the question whether such enormous generalizations are not the product of over-selective sampling and insufficient consideration of the vast amount of unexplored eighteenth-century autobiographical material that exists. It is risky, it seems to me, to take Roger North, as Morris does, as representative of "the best standard consciousness of the age." North's autobiography suits Morris's thesis well, for it is indeed, as we are told, "about what one would expect of an intelligent but not deeply introspective lawyer today," and "Roger North does not conceive of his life as an object of contemplation." [12] Quite so; but should we not be equally justified in taking the

many dozens of uncontemplative and unintrospective autobiographies of intelligent and successful British lawyers
which have appeared in the twentieth century—that of,
say, Lord Chancellor Maugham, whose "sensibility" was so
unlike that of his brother Somerset—as representative of
the standard modern consciousness?

As for Gibbon, it seems to me that Mr. Morris misses
the whole point of that great autobiography. Gibbon's
autobiography, Morris says, exemplifies "the magnificent
power of his culture to contain bitter experience." But
how, after all, did we come to know—what is certainly
true—that Gibbon was well acquainted with bitter experience? Only, of course, through the medium of the autobiography itself, through the profoundly sombre ground-
tone that is constantly heard beneath the polished ironic
surface of that magnificent work. Somehow or other, the
Autobiography has, after all, failed to "contain" that
bitterness; instead, it has communicated it; and it would
be very naive to think that, with a great artist like Gibbon,
it communicates it in spite of the writer's intentions.
When Gibbon tells us that "I sighed as a lover; I obeyed
as a son," Mr. Morris tells us, "we sense that he did not
sigh very deeply nor obey very reluctantly." [13] That is
what we are expected to sense at first reading, certainly;
but I doubt that this passage would have remained indel-
ibly engraved in the minds of generations of readers if we
did not presently sense a great deal more in it than that.
Nor is it just to take Samuel Johnson as the exemplar of
grim, Stoic, frightened repression of the emotions en-
gendered by loneliness and alienation—Johnson who, even
in a place as public as the preface to a monumental
Dictionary of the English Language, could insert so inti-

mate a piece of autobiography as "I may surely be contented without the praise of perfection, which, if I could obtain, in this gloom of solitude, what would it avail me? I have protracted my work till most of those whom I wished to please have sunk into the grave, and success and miscarriage are empty sounds: I therefore dismiss it with frigid tranquillity, having little to fear or hope from censure or from praise." This sort of thing, I am afraid, is still the old Victorian attempt to impose a preconceived pattern on the eighteenth century—perhaps because the Victorians were a little nervous of its complexity and exuberance, and wanted it brought under control. The only way for the student to break through the bonds of that pattern is to read extensively in eighteenth-century texts, not least in the wealth of autobiographical ones, whose abundance in itself amply demonstrates that the eighteenth-century "soul" was quite as much concerned as that of the nineteenth and twentieth centuries with the struggle "to find and be itself."

How Much Should a Biographer Tell?
Some Eighteenth-Century Views

JAMES L. CLIFFORD / Columbia University

When choosing the topic for this essay, I had no idea how pertinent it would be in 1967—with the Kennedy-Manchester controversy monopolizing the newspapers and periodicals. A *Newsweek* cover contains Mrs. Kennedy's perturbed face and the heading "Privacy vs. History." The *Saturday Review* devotes the large part of an issue to the argument, and has five separate articles approaching the matter from every angle—personal, historical, legal—and categorically states that this is "the greatest literary controversy of the century." [1]

In 1966 it was another outburst, this time in England, over Lord Moran's revelations concerning Churchill's last years. Here was a doctor revealing the secrets of the sick room, and horror in professional circles was widespread. Indeed, Lord Moran was publicly rebuked by the British Medical Association.

Of course, the fact that Lord Moran was a practicing physician introduced a special element into the controversy. Many people feel strongly that, by the very nature of their profession, doctors, lawyers, and clergymen can never tell what they know. Of course, secretaries, nurses,

generals, admirals, statesmen and politicians have a perfect right to get their recollections into print as speedily as
possible. Secret military and political conversations may
be disclosed, and psychiatric assessments by rank amateurs,
but not authoritative evidence concerning a great man's
health.

Lord Moran "has set an evil example," The Earl of
Birkenhead insisted,[2] and Lord Chandos added: "It is a
pity that reticence is no longer counted amongst the
modern virtues. That a doctor should disclose so many
medical details would seem to a layman to violate the tradition of one of the noblest professions." [3] The secrets of
the consulting room, the noble Lord continued, "should
be almost as closely guarded as those of the confessional."
A newspaper cartoon depicted a physician examining a
patient with a stethoscope and saying "Just say 99—and
it's not for publication."

Although special emphasis was placed on the medical
aspect, that was only one side. Lord Moran's repeating of
casual conversations on a variety of other subjects, without
securing permission from those who were quoted, stirred
up a storm of protest. "The wholesale reporting of private
conversations transgresses the canons of good manners,"
Lord Chandos reiterated.[4] If such reporting without permission continues, he added, "the private life of public
men will become intolerable, and only Trappists will hold
high office of state with equanimity."

Another central point was the inevitable financial success of such volumes. What chiefly irked a writer in the
London *Daily Mirror* was the fact that Lord Moran was
making money "by telling a tale that is distasteful and
repugnant to the widow, Lady Churchill, and to the son,

Mr. Randolph Churchill, and is published against their wishes." [5] And one cause of some of the unhappiness about William Manchester's controversial account was its inevitable financial success.

Defenders have been as vociferous in pointing out the importance to history of establishing the truth as speedily as possible. William Manchester was applauded for his refusal to allow the family's personal feelings to influence strict relation of fact, and Lord Moran's volume has been called, by a writer in the *British Medical Journal,* "a valuable contribution to the history of our times." [6] "Accuracy in the relating of history is the first need," one correspondent insists, and another adds "there is some advantage in publishing records of this kind while some of the people are alive and can answer as they think fit." [7] Lord Moran "should surely be congratulated on risking the condemnation of conventional opinion in the interest of historical truth." To the claim that intimate details should be exposed only after the subject has been dead for some time, the question is asked: Why allow a mass of untruths and erroneous guesses to remain unchallenged, while truth has to wait for a quarter of a century?

Here, then, in these two recent episodes is epitomized an age-old problem for the biographer, or for the diarist considering publishing his records. How much should he tell? Or, more properly, perhaps, how much can he tell? For the benefit of posterity must he give all the ascertainable facts? Or does good taste demand rigid censorship? Must he have complete authorization from his subject's family and friends before anything personal can be made public or any judgment formed (the efforts of a daughter to suppress an historical work critical of her father have recently been in the news).[8] Or are there gradations of decorum, depending upon how long after the death of a great man the biographer is writing? Apparently some people think that details which are taboo immediately after may be made public years later, and what may still be objectionable after two decades can safely be published a hundred years later. In other words, definitive history can be written only after all the participants, their relatives and companions, are dead.

These are the questions everyone is asking today. Were they being posed in the eighteenth century? Were there the same outcries, the same arguments, the same differences of opinion in Alexander Pope's time? Or are we more sensitive? Or merely much freer? The purpose of this essay is to attempt some hasty generalizations.

Basically the topic has two distinct parts, and at the start it may be well to define terms. The words "how much," for example, may be interpreted in different ways. They may refer merely to quantity. How many little insignificant details should be packed into a biography? Or, to put it another way, how big a book will the public accept? Does it really matter whether we know where X was on such and such a day? Or whether he had apple pie for dessert on the occasion of his dining with his great rival Y? What details are significant, and what not? Particularly for modern biographers, when the amount of available detail is enormous, this matter of how much to quote and how many little incidents to leave out becomes crucial.

Then there is the other possible meaning, which is concerned with ethics. How deeply should a biographer delve into his subject's private life? How fully should personal secrets and idiosyncrasies be revealed? If the biographer knows about discreditable actions by his subject, must he describe them fully? This is the central theme of most modern discussions.

The technical question of quantitative telling of personal anecdotes did not become central until late in the eighteenth century. There was simply no discussion of the problem, at least in any significant amount. To be sure, there were some side-remarks occasionally about triviality. Roger North, as we shall see, did appear to have some worries, and he cut out some anecdotes in his manuscripts. Owen Ruffhead, when reviewing Jortin's *Life of Erasmus* in the *Monthly Review* for October 1758, certainly shows that by that time there was some awareness of the sad results of indiscriminate publication:

As the business of biographical writing, however, consists principally in the art of *compiling,* the seeming facility of the employment, has induced many laborious drones to commence biographers, who have neither been blest with genius, taste, or learning. They have collected materials without discernment, put them together without order, and commented upon them without judgment.

These industrious drudges, equal to any fatigue themselves, seem to imagine that their readers can never be tired. Their writings are like old women's stories, in which we do not lose a single *How d'ye do?* They, no doubt, think it the office of a faithful historian, not to omit the most trivial anecdote; and they often insult our patience with tedious relations, as uninteresting as if they were to acquaint us—That on such an hour, of such a day, in such a year, the Hero of their endless tale sat down, to pair [sic] his nails.[9]

But nowhere can one find any serious analysis of such matters as why one anecdote is worth remembering, and another one not, or exactly the significance of some little point. It was not until after Boswell had shown what could be done by piling up a huge collection of anecdotes illustrating the life of a single individual that there was any such discussion. And even then there was little significant critical analysis of the decisions a biographer must make when judging the relevance of evidence. Usually the point merely centered around apparent triviality. Still, by the end of the century the matter did provide subject matter for satires and take-offs. It was easy to burlesque the new biographical completeness by producing a series of vapid, unrelated stories.[10]

But quantity and triviality are really not the central problem. Of much more importance is the ethical question. How much more intimate personal material should a biographer include? And when may he safely do it? For this I should like to consider separately the two halves of the century. Until 1750, so far as I can see, there was very little consideration of the problem. It was simply not a live issue. To be sure, I base this conclusion largely on haphazard reading, on long years of curious dipping, though I am relieved to say that it is confirmed by other scholars whose advice I have sought. Before the middle of the century it is rare to find serious criticism of any kind having to do with the art of biography. Addison and Steele and their many imitators scarcely ever touch on the problem. In thousands of private letters there is never a reference. There are no magazine comments or special pamphlets on the subject.

There were, of course, a few peripheral comments. Addison in 1716, in his *Freeholder,* No. 35, protested against the Grub Street biographers, who watch for the death of a great man, and in order to "make a penny" sacrifice "the secrets of the dead to the curiosity of the living." [11] Lives of great men, Addison insisted, cannot be written with exactness until long after their deaths. The reserved, sensitive Addison was obviously in the same camp with Thomas Sprat, who, in his life of the poet Cowley in 1668 refused to quote from any of his subject's personal letters.[12] Nothing of this sort, he insisted, should ever be made public. Such a conviction represented the conservative position. But not everyone wholly agreed.

By the late seventeenth century there was some feeling that personal details might be revealed, if caution were used. Nevertheless, too much should not be made of the biographical curiosity shown by such people as John Aubrey. His brief lives were intended for the eyes of Anthony à Wood alone. They were not written for publication. Even if Aubrey did insist that what he was supplying represented "the naked and plaine trueth," he requested Wood, after his perusal of the sketches, to "make a castration," and "to sew on some figge leaves." [13] He recognized that what he had written was not "fit to lett flie abroad, till about 30 years hence; for the author and the persons (like medlars) ought to be rotten first."

Even Roger North, who we know thought long and hard about the genre, had nothing significant to say about these crucial problems. In his long manuscript "General Preface," apparently intended to precede the lives of his brothers, but even to this day not wholly in print, he never considered the problem.[14] Although he has much to say about the importance of full coverage in biography, about the dangers and reasons for slanted accounts, about proper ways of collecting trustworthy evidence, all of which shows him a worthy forerunner of Johnson and Boswell,

he avoids the question of ethics. Nor does he really face
the matter of exploring personal secrets in the printed
Lives.

Of course, North always insisted on the necessity of
telling the truth. "A life should be a picture; which cannot be good, if the peculiar features, whereby the subject
is distinguished from all others, are left out. Nay, scars
and blemishes, as well as beauties, ought to be expressed;
otherwise, it is but an outline filled up with lillies and
roses." [15] For him, however, there was no great problem
since his three brothers had generally been so virtuous.
What faults he saw in them he records quite honestly
(Dudley's dealings with the courtesans in Venice, Francis's
drunken ride, or the story of the rhinoceros).[16] To be sure,
either he or his son, who later arranged for the publication of the lives, did take out a number of anecdotes about
his elder brother which showed him in a bad light. There
was the story about his admission to the Middle Temple,
and of his quibbling with the college barber.[17] But there is
no evidence that Roger North seriously anticipated any
accusations of having revealed improprieties. He was more
worried about possible claims that he had included too
much trivia.

As Mr. Peter Millard has pointed out to me, what one
might call the influence of the Royal Society is important
in Roger North's work. He seemed to regard himself almost as a scientist, noting the habits of men with the same
exactness as, say, a zoologist brings to the study of animals.
Such an attitude obviously encouraged him to reveal all.
In an unpublished passage in one of the original versions
of his life of the Lord Keeper, Roger remarked "these may
seem triviall passages, not worth Remembring but being

Exactly true, are part of yᵉ Naturall history of Mankind, wᶜʰ is Every ones Interest to know." ¹⁸ His determination to assemble an almost complete record may be seen by the fact that the first manuscript version runs to ten volumes.

Although one can find no specific comment from North, there is ample evidence that he refused to take a repressive position as to the handling of family papers. The very writing of the life of his brother, John, was an invasion of privacy, for Roger well knew that by doing so he was going counter to the wishes of his subject. John had openly expressed horror at leaving any memorial of his life behind, had refused to sit for a portrait, and had left the strictest instructions to burn all his papers.¹⁹ Yet Roger unhesitatingly laid bare the life of his brother to the public, and carefully included the Doctor's notes which had chanced to escape the flames. In one of the manuscript versions, to be sure, he rationalized his action by pointing out that it had been his brother Francis, and not he, who had promised to destroy the papers.

The inevitable question of why there was such a complete lack of significant criticism of biography in the first half of the eighteenth century is not easy to answer. On the surface, conditions might appear to have been propitious. This was the high point of neoclassical satire, with its emphasis on colorful individual characters. "The proper study of mankind is man," Alexander Pope insisted, and everyone seems to have agreed. Why, then, no serious consideration of life writing? This was the period of immense expansion of critical media—of the beginnings of the newspaper and the increase in periodical publications. Yet there was almost complete silence on one of the themes which interests us most and which fills our newspapers.

Why? The answer is not easy, but I should like to try to suggest some reasons. In the first place, no one realized that there was a problem. Most life-writers of the day seemed almost instinctively to have known what to do, depending upon what tradition they were in. The purveyor of ethical examples merely strung together a series of edifying anecdotes.[20] The writer of candid memoirs or confessions knew that there had to be some softening and some censoring. One can infer what was required from the Prefaces to some of Defoe's novels, where the illusion is created that the printed work had real origins. Thus the "editor" of *Moll Flanders* claimed to have put the account "in modester words than she told it at first"; and "some of the vicious part of her life, which could not be modestly told, is quite left out"; with other parts "very much shortened."[21] The "Author's Preface" to *Roxana* made the point that it had been "necessary to conceal names and persons," and that all imaginable care had been taken "to keep clear of indecencies, and immodest expressions." All of this was an accepted part of the type.

No one quite knew what straight biography was, or what it should be. Most people, I suspect, regarded it merely as one technique of history. Lives were written by historians. Some may have wondered, like North, if it should not be a scientific discipline—for the analytical study of mankind. But it was *not* widely recognized as a literary genre. In practice, by the early eighteenth century there were two easily recognizable types of life-writing: the formal panegyric, which stemmed from pious saints' lives of the middle ages; and the nasty, scurrilous journalistic bits of debunking of the type turned out by "The Unspeakable Curll." Nobody took either of these seriously as works of art. There was practically nothing in between, for the balanced, revealing type of life had simply not yet been invented.[22]

Some of the eulogies, like those of Izaak Walton, might have had delightful human touches, but there was never any pretense that they represented three-dimensional portraiture. And some of the criminal lives and scandalous memoirs may have been thoroughly researched and smoothly written, but again nobody for a moment thought of them as an art form. Consequently there was nothing serious to say about them.

If questioned, almost everyone would have parroted Plutarch's arguments about complete fidelity and truth in history and in great men's lives. Typical is Robert Shiels, who in the *Lives of the Poets* published in 1753, asserted that he was dedicated to impartiality, "which we have endeavoured to observe throughout this work." [23] Shiels insisted that "in biographical writing, the first and most essential principle is candour, which no reverence for the memory of the dead, nor affection for the virtues of the living should violate." And Lord Orrery's life of Swift was praised because he had tried to show the man as he really was, both his virtues and his "many failings." Again and again one can find this kind of general statement. David Mallet, William Ayre, William Oldys—all say much the same thing.[24] Yet there was little curiosity as to the kinds of problems facing a biographer who tried to present the whole truth about a contemporary. How can this neglect be explained?

The easiest way is to cite the general shift of sensibility in the eighteenth century. In the earlier portion, in what we generally categorize as the peak of neoclassical reliance on tradition, there was widespread acceptance of what we call the theory of genres. Only certain classical types were officially admired, and these in well-known gradations. Epic and tragedy, of course, came at the top, with lyric and satire farther down the scale. Nowhere in such listings would one ever find biography. Moreover, inherent in the neoclassical creed was a preference for the general as opposed to individual idiosyncrasies. Pope may often have been as morbid and depressed as any romantic poet, but he did not think such matters the proper subjects of poetry. The image which he presents in his work is a public one. Man is interesting as part of general Nature, not as a thwarted split personality. In consequence, one might say, the climate of opinion was not suitable for biographical experimentation. But during the second half of the century a radical change occurred. Something fundamental happened, which fostered the rise of revealing biography.

Basic was the overwhelming influence of Locke, both in psychology and in the rights of the individual. Increasingly, the emphasis was upon human behavior and upon the importance of ordinary experience.[25] According to this kind of interpretation the reversal was allied to the coming of romanticism. Following the gradual breakdown of classical standards, emphasis shifted from the general to the specific, from the objective to the subjective; from the conviction that man was only a subordinate facet in a stable social and religious order to the introspective individualism of the next century.[26] Biography can thus be interpreted as a romantic genre, a product of the new insistence on looking into a man's heart and motives. From this point of view it is all quite simple and understandable.

Yet somehow this explanation strikes me as too pat—

too easy and superficial. There is always the nagging suspicion that there must have been other contributing factors which have not been adequately explored. If the shift to detailed biography is basically romantic, then why was Samuel Johnson the major moving force behind the change? Have we been wrong about him from the start? When choosing preromantic writers who preceded Wordsworth and Coleridge, should Beers and Phelps and the older critics have stressed Johnson rather than Collins, Gray and Cowper? It is an intriguing thought, but to follow it further would lead me far afield. I will gladly leave this byway to others to explore.

Undoubtedly the rise of intimate biography is in some way connected with the shift to romanticism, but it is even more closely allied to an increase of interest in realism in fiction. When searching for basic reasons behind the change, we might more profitably concentrate upon this. The new life-writing which stressed wealth of detail, color and depth of character, followed closely on the rise of the English novel. Indeed, the two seem inextricably interwoven. Richardson and Fielding in the 1740's showed how fascinating individual character could be, when portrayed in psychological depth. From this it must have been natural to ask: If fictional characters can be made to appear exactly like real men and women, cannot people who have actually lived be described with the same richness and depth as fictional creations? If the novelist is able to suggest levels of psychological conflict in his characters, may it not be possible to give comparable richness to accounts of individuals who have actually lived? Undoubtedly this is a crucial point. Whether or not it is the basic reason, can never be proved.

But there is no reason to carry this further. What is important is the fact that even with all the widening of interest in biography and the increased skill of the practitioners, it was some time before there was any sign of serious consideration of the main ethical problems involved. One might almost say that not until after Boswell did the general public become seriously involved with such matters. Consequently there is need to trace in some detail the first stirrings of this interest.

Here Samuel Johnson is a central figure. But since so much has been written about Johnson and the art of biography—by Bergen Evans, and recently by the late John Butt—I will not attempt an overall analysis.[27] Nevertheless a few remarks should be made. A convenient starting place is Johnson's *Rambler* essay No. 60, in October 1750. As a practicing biographer himself, Johnson had undoubtedly been mulling over many of the problems involved. Although there had been few ethical considerations in his pieces for the *Gentleman's Magazine*, since largely what he was doing there was condensing and reworking already-published material, in his *Life of Savage* in 1744 he had been faced with major decisions. How much should he tell about his friend's vices, his psychopathic weaknesses, and his erratic existence? How openly should he take Savage's side? Ought he to suppress the discreditable episodes? Of course, there is no way for us to tell how much he did suppress. This much is certain. Enough of Savage's masochistic pathology did come through to make Johnson's life the first genuinely three-dimensional biography, with psychological overtones, in the English language.[28]

In theory Johnson was convinced of the value of minute

details properly used, and of the need of showing all sides. He saw clearly that the mere presentation of a chronological series of actions is not enough to produce an effective word portrait. "More knowledge," he stressed in his *Rambler* essay, "may be gained of a man's real character, by a short conversation with one of his servants, than from a formal and studied narrative, begun with his pedigree, and ended with his funeral." [29] Yet Johnson was just as aware of the dangers of uncritical use of trivial anecdotes. How valuable is it for us to know about the irregularity of Addison's pulse?

That Johnson was deeply committed to the doctrine of strict truth in historical relations cannot be doubted. Edmond Malone records that Johnson

was so great a lover of truth that no consideration could make him deviate from it. In relating circumstances that had fallen within his own knowledge and that of other friends, Sir Joshua Reynolds has told me, that some of them would sometimes add somewhat by the way of embelishment—but he would never suffer it; 'What you mention (he would say) would make the story better, but it was not so.' [30]

And in the *Rambler* essay he replies to those who think it an act of piety to hide the faults or failings of their friends, "If we owe regard to the memory of the dead, there is yet more respect to be paid to knowledge, to virtue, and to truth." In later pronouncements, both oral and in print, Johnson continued to stress the importance of strict historical relation.

On the other hand, he was well aware of the pressures on a biographer, and he was not always consistent in his later pronouncements. Quite clearly he could not make up his mind as to the moral considerations involved. At different times, so Boswell shows in one very important paragraph in the *Life,* Johnson could argue cogently on opposite sides.

Talking of biography, I said, in writing a life, a man's peculiarities should be mentioned, because they mark his character. JOHNSON. 'Sir, there is no doubt as to peculiarities: the question is, whether a man's vices should be mentioned; for instance, whether it should be mentioned that Addison and Parnell drank too freely; for people will probably more easily indulge in drinking from knowing this; so that more ill may be done by the example, than good by telling the whole truth.' Here was an instance of his varying from himself in talk; for when Lord Hailes and he sat one morning calmly conversing in my house at Edinburgh, I well remember that Dr. Johnson maintained, that 'If a man is to write *A Panegyrick,* he may keep vices out of sight; but if he professes to write *A Life,* he must represent it really as it was:' and when I objected to the danger of telling that Parnell drank to excess, he said, that 'it would produce an instructive caution to avoid drinking, when it was seen, that even the learning and genius of Parnell could be debased by it.' And in the Hebrides he maintained, as appears from my 'Journal,' that a man's intimate friend should mention his faults, if he writes his life.[31]

In his *Life of Addison,* a few years later, Johnson succinctly summed up the crucial problem connected with the recording of the life of a contemporary person. "The necessity of complying with times and of sparing persons is the great impediment of biography. . . . What is known can seldom be immediately told." [32] And even though by waiting and by censorship much may be lost, that is surely better than that "by wanton merriment and unseasonable detection a pang should be given to a widow, a daughter, a brother, or a friend." (Does this sound strangely familiar

—like the problems of William Manchester?) Johnson even went so far as to admit that "As the process of these narratives is now bringing me among my contemporaries I begin to feel myself, 'walking upon ashes under which the fire is not extinguished,' and coming to the time of which it will be proper rather to say 'nothing that is false, than all that is true.' "

Faced, then, with the immediate problem of possible family resentment and friends' disapproval, Johnson reluctantly confessed himself willing to postpone telling the whole truth. But for how long? And just what kind of details should be temporarily censored? Johnson fails to tell us. He obstinately refused to grapple with such professional decisions, perhaps preferring, as in his literary criticism, to avoid general rules and to evaluate each case separately. Biography, like all art for him, must please and instruct, but there is no way to set up guide lines to tell exactly how this may be accomplished.

Johnson, then, is the first modern critic to show any deep awareness of the basic problems we are discussing. If he does not provide satisfactory answers, it may be that none can be given. Certainly no one else in his day seriously canvassed the problem. William Mason, in his very popular *Life of Gray* in 1775 certainly did not. He makes clear that all he is doing is selecting examples from his subject's correspondence in order to show various aspects of Gray's character—chiefly illustrating his career as scholar and poet.[33] At one point he says that he intends to select "those parts which, I imagine, will be most likely either to inform or amuse the reader." And we know that he ruthlessly cut, rearranged, and mangled the correspondence, sometimes even combining parts of a number of letters from different dates into one ostensibly unified letter. The whole truth was certainly not his aim.

At the risk of being immediately challenged, I am tempted to say that there was nothing comparable to modern arguments until the furor resulting from the publicizing of intimate private details concerning Dr. Johnson, shortly after his death. Then for the first time in England, surely, public curiosity about a great man was gratified by the appearance of a huge mass of very intimate and revealing material. With the publication of Johnson's deeply personal prayers and meditations, of the many short lives, which contained records of his casual remarks and angry denunciations, his conversation with his friends, ethical considerations naturally became paramount. It is not surprising that strong protests should have been registered. What was occurring, many felt, not only showed lack of taste, but also severely injured Johnson's reputation. Here, then, was a situation very like those in our time.

Boswell is now acknowledged to be one of the world's greatest biographers and his works are accepted as masterpieces. We tend to forget that in his own day he was subjected to the same kind of abuse as is now heaped on Lord Moran and William Manchester. While not insisting on comparable merit, the point is inescapable that honest, revealing biography inevitably does stir up controversy and anger. To tell even large portions of truth is sure to be unpalatable to some of those who are described.

It should be stressed that Boswell did not himself attempt to give the whole truth. For many readers in the late eighteenth century it must have seemed as if he told everything he knew about his subject. Yet we know this

was not so. As a result of the discovery of Boswell's ar-
chives and of the complete manuscript of the *Life,* we can
see how much he left out, and how hard he tried not to
irritate living people. For various reasons—possibly to
insure a more consistent portrait of Johnson—Boswell
omitted a good deal which would have rendered his account even more amusing and revealing. For example, he
left out an apparently authentic account secured from
Edmund Hector of a time when Johnson as a young man
may have been drunk, as well as a later scene when he
insisted on having another bottle of wine. Boswell refused
to pass on Johnson's decision, a year after Tetty's death,
to seek a second wife. Not included was a sensational
interview Boswell had with Mrs. Desmoulins where the
topic was Johnson's sexual capacities and false rumors of
his impotence. Labelled by Boswell "Tacenda"—"Keep
hidden"—this journal entry is still not in print.[34]

In order not to hurt others, Boswell in the *Tour to the
Hebrides* softened harsh remarks about Sir Alexander
Macdonald, though enough remained to bring him close
to a duel.[35] In the *Life* he left out a number of cutting
remarks about Bennet Langton, and a highly diverting
scene of a dinner with Molly Aston's husband, Captain
Brodie. Boswell bowed to the wishes of Percy and Reynolds and did not mention Johnson's help with certain
of their publications.[36]

At the very last minute he cancelled a page in the *Life*
which had included some remarks on conjugal infidelity,
because Windham and others thought them indelicate,
although he lamented to Malone that they were "mighty
good stuff." [37] Even after publication he was ready to
make changes to ease the resentment of persons who felt

insulted by his revelations. Witness the changes in the second edition of the *Tour*. Indeed, Boswell once claimed to have suppressed everything that he thought would hurt any living person.[38]

Despite all this censorship and consideration for other's feelings, there was still enough intimate material in Boswell's accounts to shock many of his readers. When the *Tour* first appeared in the autumn of 1785 there was a storm of protest. The *Morning Post* on October 1 commented: "Had Dr. Johnson been blessed with the gift of *second-sight,* how it would have tortured him to have known the base advantages which have been taken of his celebrity to make money." On the 8th Johnson was compared to a dead whale cast up on the sands at Leith, and made a show of by his younger Scots friend. And throughout October and November there were continued hits at Boswell for his anecdotes.

Horace Walpole, in a letter to Conway, called the *Tour* a "most absurd enormous book . . . It is the story of a mountebank and his zany." [39] According to Michael Lort, Edmund Burke "fell hard upon" Boswell for the absurdities in his book, and John Wilkes told him that "he had wounded Johnson with his pocket pistol & was about to despatch him with his blunderbuss when it should be let off." [40] The popular satirist, Peter Pindar, found Boswell a perfect target for derision:

> I see thee stuffing, with a hand uncouth,
> An old dry'd whiting in thy Johnson's mouth;
> And lo! I see, with all his might and main,
> Thy Johnson spit the whiting out again.
> Rare anecdotes! 'tis anecdotes like these,
> That bring thee glory, and the million please!

> On these, shall future times delighted stare,
> Thou charming haberdasher of small ware.[41]

The story is told that Lord Monboddo, when asked what he thought of Boswell, replied: "Before I read his Book [the *Tour*] I thought he was a Gentleman who had the misfortune to be mad; I now think he is a mad man who has the misfortune not to be a Gentleman." [42] But the most severe reprobation came from Mrs. Montagu, "Queen of the Bluestockings." Irritated by Boswell's recording of Johnson's unfavorable reaction to her book on Shakespeare, she replied to Mrs. Piozzi's own embarrassed disclaimer of a similar opinion with obvious displeasure.

However I will confess my mortification was mitigated by the very moderate degree of credit I gave to all Mr Boswell had ascribed to Dr Johnson. In the first place poor Mr Boswell is very often in that condition in which men are said to see double; perhaps in such circumstance their hearing is as much disordered; & then what is still stronger objection to his testimony, he could hardly have had any motive for his publication but that of making it the vehicle of censure & scandal. Certainly it does not contain any thing that could do honour to the memory of his deceased friend. . . . Would any man who wish'd his friend to have the respect of posterity exhibit all his little caprices, his unhappy infirmities, his singularities; these were excused by friends & intimates who [?] are soften'd by experienced kindness & demonstrated virtues but they disgrace a character to a reader as wens and warts would do a statue or Portrait to a spectator.[43]

Mrs. Montagu, indeed, found the whole tendency of modern biography displeasing.

May this new invented mode of disgracing the dead & calumniating ye living perish with the short lived work of Master Boswell, but the effect & consequences of such an example of

Biography makes me shudder, as better pens, with still worse intentions, may adopt it, & the Grave be no longer the place where the Wicked cease from troubling, & the holiest Christian, the sincerest Patriot will not be sure he may not after his death be made to talk blasphemy or utter treason.

The reviewer in the *Monthly Review*, Samuel Badcock, while admitting that the publication had afforded him much entertainment, was a trifle puzzled as to what position he should take.

The general maxim, that trifles become of serious consequence when connected with men of illustrious names, is very often carried too far by their partial admirers; but when a great man is exhibited in those moments in which he forgets his dignity, we rather blame the historian who records his weakness, than the hero, who in common life is no more than a common man. If, however, the hero is pleased to see himself reduced to the level of frail mortality, who will then find fault with the historian? If Dr. Johnson was satisfied to have the foolish speeches he made, and the perverse things he did, recorded with fidelity;—if on reviewing them, he pronounced them to be faithful representations of his principles, his manners, and his conversation, who will blame Mr. Boswell?[44]

Just the same, in looking forward to what was still to come, the reviewer advised Boswell

We wish him to copy the example of Plutarch, who, though he followed his heroes to the recesses of private life, and exhibited them in the hours of social ease, yet generally left in the shade what tended to diminish their greatness, or sully their virtues.

For conservative persons, just as for the noble Lords who were so shocked by Lord Moran's disclosures, the prospect of invasion of privacy, as practiced by the new biographers, was more than frightening. James Beattie

summed up this point of view in a letter to Sir William
Forbes. While admitting that Boswell had "meant no
harm," he indicated that he thought many things in the
Tour "injudicious." And he added, "Johnson's faults were
balanced by many and great virtues; and when that is the
case, the virtues only should be remembered, and the
faults entirely forgotten." [45] Biography should commemo-
rate, not delineate.

With the appearance in March 1786 of Mrs. Thrale-
Piozzi's *Anecdotes of Dr. Johnson,* the chorus of disapproval grew more vociferous. Of course, as with Boswell's
Tour, there were favorable notices and some praise for
the entertainment which such books did provide. But
there was continual harping on the same old complaints.
"This new-fashioned biography," Hannah More wrote to
her sister, "seems to value itself upon perpetuating every
thing that is injurious and detracting." [46] Dr. Burney in
the *Monthly Review* began by quoting Cicero's diatribe
against Anthony for relating things told in secret, and
continued: "What admirer of the moral excellencies, and
of the extensive learning of the late Samuel Johnson, can
forbear feeling the same indignation, and expressing it
with equal warmth, when they behold his former friends
exposing his failings and his weaknesses, to the curious,
yet fastidious eye of the Public?" [47]

The reviewer in *The English Review,* along with high
praise for Mrs. Piozzi's penetration and good sense, could
not refrain from repeating the same complaint about
the "indiscreet and dishonorable conduct" of Dr. Johnson's "professed friends and admirers, in exposing to the
ridicule of the world all the absurdities and follies which
fell from his tongue, in his weak, wicked, and mad mo-

ments." [48] He added: "A distinguished character may be allowed some peculiarities and oddities, but there is no occasion to transfer them to the list of his virtues." Over and over there was registered astonishment that Johnson's biographers appeared intent on exposing "the failings and weaknesses of their friend." [49] In *Bozzy and Piozzi,* Peter Pindar came back to the attack with another hilarious burlesque of the new insistence on giving all the little facts about their hero. He imagined the two biographers engaged in an argument, using some of the silliest anecdotes from their works. Here is a sample:

BOZZY

Who would have said a word about Sam's wig;
Or told the story of the pease and pig?
Who would have told a tale so very flat,
Of Frank the Black, and Hodge the mangy cat?

MADAME PIOZZI

Good me! you're grown at once confounded tender
Of Doctor Johnson's fame a fierce defender:
I'm sure you've mention'd many a pretty story
Not much redounding to the Doctor's glory.
Now for a saint upon us you would palm him—
First murder the poor man, and then enbalm him! [50]

The English Review kept up the adverse criticism:

The character of Dr. Johnson has been exposed to much ridicule, by the injudicious minuteness of his biographers. They have pursued him into every retreat, and exposed him in every situation to the public eye. The veil which human weakness requires has been wantonly drawn aside, and the nakedness of their idol discovered. Every consideration must give way to the voracity of the anecdote-hunter; who without any object but the satisfaction of his appetite, swallows and disembogues. . . .[51]

One could go on and on, quoting the objections to what was generally now known as the new biography, and all this before Boswell's huge *Life of Johnson* appeared. So Vicesimus Knox complained: "Biography is every day descending from its dignity. Instead of an instructive recital, it is becoming an instrument to the mere gratification of an impertinent, not to say malignant, curiosity. . . ."[52] Such indecent exposure, Knox insisted, could be of little use to the multitude. The common reader, he felt, would, on the example of great men's weaknesses, give up the contest, and "shelter his surrender under the name and authority of the defunct philosopher."

There is even some evidence that Boswell was in later years not received in certain circles with the same pleasure as formerly. Percy later claimed that he was "studiously excluded" from decent company, and the wife of Archibald Alison, in complaining about Boswell's "gross gossipation," commented "how well he deserves what he daily meets with that of people shutting their doors against him as they would against any other wild Beast."[53]

Of course, Boswell's *magnum opus* in 1791 was subjected to similar violent attack. For many readers there was the customary split—between amused pleasure over many entertaining portions, and a kind of shock over the intimate details which were revealed. To list all the attacks would require another essay. There were further pressures on Boswell to expunge remarks of other people— for example, this time by Alexander Fraser Tyler, later

Lord Woodhouselee [54]—and the same objections to his indiscreet revelations of casual remarks made in private. Anna Laetitia Barbauld commented: "It is like going to Ranelagh; you meet all your acquaintance: but it is a base and a mean thing to bring thus every idle word into judgement—the judgement of the public." [55] Bishop Percy, long afterward, put this attitude quite simply: "It is surely an exception more than venial to violate one of the first and most sacred laws of society, by publishing private and unguarded conversation of unsuspecting company into which he was accidentally admitted." [56] And Robert Anderson called it a "violation of the confidence of society." [57]

On the other hand, by the time of the *Life,* many readers were quite ready to accept the new approach with enthusiasm. The issue of how much a biographer should tell had finally come to life. Here was something about which critics might disagree, as we do today. At last the crucial problems of the biographer were out in the open. Even though the next century would see a temporary return to stress on reticence and good taste,[58] the possibilities of wide coverage, both psychological and factual, were now apparent. As a sample, I might quote from one review of the *Life.* Ralph Griffiths in the *Monthly Review,* for January 1792 openly confronted the question of how much evidence should be given. Some objectors, he pointed out, claim that by giving too much a biography can become dull.

On the other hand, an approver will contend, that where the biographer has for his subject the life and sentiments of so eminent an instructor of mankind as Samuel Johnson, and so immense a store-house of mental treasure to open and disclose to the eager curiosity of rational and laudable inquiry, there can be no just exception taken against the number and variety of the objects exhibited. He will ask 'What conversation could have passed, where so great a genius presided, at which every man of learning and taste would not wish to have been present, or, at least, to have it faithfully reported to him?' To the reporter, would he not say 'Give us *all*; suppress nothing; lest, in rejecting that which, in your estimation, may seem to be of inferior value, you unwarily throw away gold with the dross.' [59]

And in evaluating Boswell's achievement, Griffiths insisted that he was among the number of readers:

who do not think that he has set before us too plenteous an entertainment; nor have we found, that, often as we have sat down to his mental feast, we have ever risen from it with a cloyed appetite.

The old emphasis on good taste, to be sure, was always present. Such readers as Samuel Whyte, the cousin of Mrs. Thomas Sheridan, kept on parroting the age-old objections. Whyte in 1799 wrote:

A great character, in worthy situations, is an object of virtuous contemplation; but that minuteness of anecdote, that ostentatious display of trifles, which we sometimes meet with, is a vicious indulgence of inquisitive impertinence; a flagrant breach of private confidence, and an infringement of the rules of good breeding.[60]

In conclusion, I fear I have not provided any clear-cut solutions. All I have been able to do is to show how little the eighteenth century thought about biographical problems, and how impossible it was for practicing life-writers to be completely honest. Even men like Boswell, who avowed adherence to the general theory of over-all truth, found it impractical to tell everything they knew.[61] There was always some point or other that had to be kept hidden, at least for awhile. But for how long? That question never could be answered with any assurance. Each instance represents a separate case. Everything appears to depend on the nature of the controversial material, the character of the subject and the idolatry of the public.

There are some types of crimes or suspicions of depravity that can scarcely be made public until long after the time described, even if then. For an inherently virtuous subject, on the other hand, the problems cluster around the sensitive feelings of his family and friends, who may object to any sort of publicity for themselves. Does the biographer, then, have to wait until everyone mentioned or quoted is dead? Or should he defy public opinion and refuse to bow to the dictates of exaggerated sensibility? Even today—as is evident from the uproar attending Lord Moran and William Manchester—we have not worked out any acceptable formula.

Certainly the predicament of such writers as Boswell and Lord Moran epitomizes a paradox of modern liberal thinking. As one London editorial aptly put it, "It is an irony that the British people, who are justly proud of their devotion to freedom of discussion, are also among the most strenuous advocates of the voluntary suppression of opinion and fact." [62] Any attempt to set down the whole truth is permissible for past ages, but not if it touches one's own affairs.

Certainly the road of the biographer who attempts a contemporary subject is difficult.[63] His basic choice is clear. No attempts at compromise are ever wholly successful. Either he will keep on good terms with all his subject's friends and relations and disappoint posterity— or he will brave the displeasure of his own day and live in hopes of eventual recognition. Happily for us a few do take the harder way.

Studies in Eighteenth-Century Autobiography and Biography: A Selected Bibliography

ROBERT E. KELLEY / *University of Iowa*

The following is a selected, not an exhaustive, list of critical and scholarly writings. It is included here to offer additional readings along the lines suggested by the essays in this volume. The selections do not include books and articles with only a passing interest in Restoration and Eighteenth-Century autobiography and biography, dissertations, and, except in certain instances, biographies of the writers in question. Further readings may be found in James L. Clifford's *Johnsonian Studies, 1887–1950: A Survey and Bibliography* (Minneapolis, 1951); Clifford and Donald J. Greene's "A Bibliography of Johnsonian Studies, 1950-1960," *Johnsonian Studies,* ed. Magdi Wahba (Cairo, 1962); and Anthony E. Brown's "Boswellian Studies: A Bibliography," *Cairo Studies in English,* ed. Magdi Wahba (Cairo, 1966). Annotation, where it seemed useful, has been provided. Cross references to general studies have been supplied in the section on individual authors.

Autobiography

1. Bates, E. Stewart. *Inside Out: An Introduction to Autobiography.* Oxford, 1936.
2. Bottrall, Margaret. *Every Man a Phoenix: Studies in Seventeenth-Century Autobiography.* London, 1958. Contains chapters on Bunyan and Baxter.

3. Clark, Arthur M. *Autobiography: Its Genesis and Phases.* Edinburgh, 1935.
4. Matthews, William, ed. *British Autobiographies: An Annotated Bibliography of British Autobiographies Published or Written Before 1951.* Berkeley and Los Angeles, 1955.
5. Morris, John N. *Versions of the Self: Studies in English Autobiography from John Bunyan to John Stuart Mill.* New York, 1966. Includes useful discussions of North, Gibbon, Bunyan, Cowper, and Boswell.
6. Shumaker, Wayne. *English Autobiography: Its Emergence, Materials, and Form.* Berkeley and Los Angeles, 1954. Cites the eighteenth century as a period of "flowering" of autobiography.
7. Starr, George. *Defoe and Spiritual Autobiography.* Princeton, 1965. Introductory chapter on spiritual autobiography in the seventeenth and eighteenth centuries.
8. Wethered, H. N. *The Curious Art of Autobiography from Benvenuto Cellini to Rudyard Kipling.* New. York, 1956. Includes material on Bunyan, Baxter, Pepys, Gibbon, Rousseau, Franklin.

Biography

RESTORATION AND EIGHTEENTH CENTURY

9. Addison, Joseph. *The Freeholder,* No. 35, 20 April 1716. Attacks Grub Street biography.
10. Aubrey, John. Letter to Anthony à Wood, 15 June 1680. Included in *Aubrey's Brief Lives,* ed. Andrew Clark. London, 1898, I, 10-11. Discusses truth in biography.
11. Dryden, John. "The Life of Plutarch," prefixed to *Plutarch's Lives, Translated from the Greek by Several Hands.* London, 1683–1686. Reprinted in John Dryden, *Of Dramatic Poesy and Other Critical Essays,* ed. George Watson. London, 1962, II, 1–13. Relation of biography to history; characteristics of biography.
12. Johnson, Samuel. *Rambler* No. 60, 13 October 1750; *Idler* Nos. 84, 24 November 1759, and 102, 29 March 1760.

13. Knox, Vicesimus. "Cursory Thoughts on Biography," *Essays Moral and Literary*. London, 1782, II, 48–52. Biography and history; brief survey of biography.

14. ————. "On the Character of Dr. Johnson and the Abuse of Biography," *Winter Evenings: or, Lucubrations on Life and Letters*. London, 1790, pp. 70–73. Argues for discreet biography.

15. North, Roger. "General Preface" to *Life of the Lord Keeper North*. First published in *Biography as an Art*, ed. James L. Clifford. New York, 1962, pp. 27–37.

16. "On Biography," *The Lady's Magazine*, XVIII (August 1787), 425. Brief testament to the moral value of biography.

NINETEENTH CENTURY

17. Cunningham, Allan. "Biographical and Critical History of the Literature of the Last Fifty Years," *The Athenaeum* (14 December 1833), pp. 851–53. Surveys the work of Boswell, James Currie, William Hayley, Malcolm Laing.

18. Stanfield, James. *Essay on the Study and Composition of Biography*. Sunderland, 1813. Deals with Boswell.

TWENTIETH CENTURY: BOOKS

19. Altick, Richard D. *Lives and Letters: A History of Literary Biography in England and America*. New York, 1965. Discusses seventeenth- and eighteenth-century biography, with special attention to Johnson and Boswell.

20. Britt, Albert. *The Great Biographers*. New York, 1936. Brief chapter on Johnson and Boswell.

21. Butt, John. *Biography in the Hands of Walton, Johnson, and Boswell*. Los Angeles, 1966.

22. Carver, George. *Alms for Oblivion: Books, Men, and Biography*. Milwaukee, 1946. Brief chapters on Walton, Fuller, Margaret Newcastle, Dryden, North, Johnson, Mason, Goldsmith, Boswell, and Malone.

23. Dunn, Waldo. *English Biography*. London, 1916. Chapter on the rise of biography in the eighteenth century.

24. Edel, Leon. *Literary Biography*. Toronto and London,

1957; republished with additions, New York, 1959. Useful section on Johnson and Boswell under heading of "subject."

25. Garraty, John A. *The Nature of Biography*. New York, 1957. Cursory survey of the development and maturation of biography in the seventeenth and eighteenth centuries.

26. Johnson, Edgar. *One Mighty Torrent: the Drama of Biography*. New York, 1937. Full sections on seventeenth- and eighteenth-century biographers, autobiographers, and memoirists.

27. Johnston, James C. *Biography: the Literature of Personality*. New York, 1927. Discusses some eighteenth-century biographers under various headings.

28. Kendall, Paul Murray. *The Art of Biography*. New York, 1965. Brief treatment of Restoration and eighteenth-century biography.

29. Longaker, Mark. *English Biography in the Eighteenth Century*. Philadelphia, 1931.

30. Nicolson, Harold. *The Development of English Biography*. London, 1927. Includes two chapters on biography from Walton through Boswell.

31. Pearson, Hesketh. *Ventilations: Being Biographical Asides*. Philadelphia, 1930. Discusses Boswell and Johnson under headings of "truth," "evasion," and "personal biography."

32. Reed, Joseph W., Jr. *English Biography in the Early Nineteenth Century 1801–1838*. New Haven, 1966. Excellent chapter on relation of Boswell to nineteenth-century biography.

33. Stauffer, Donald A. *The Art of Biography in Eighteenth-Century England*. 2 vols. Princeton, 1941. Extensive treatment of the subject, though not well-organized. The second volume is an alphabetical list of eighteenth-century biographies; its reliability has been questioned.

34. _____. *English Biography Before 1700*. Cambridge, Mass., 1930. Discusses at some length Restoration biography and autobiography.

35. Thayer, William R. *The Art of Biography*. New York, 1920. Brief discussion of Johnson and Boswell.

36. Trevelyan, G. M. *Biography: A Reader's Guide*. London, 1947.

37. Wellek, René. *The Rise of English Literary History*. Chapel Hill, 1941. Excellent treatment of collective biography and biographical dictionaries.

TWENTIETH CENTURY: ESSAYS

38. Benson, A. C. "The Art of the Biographer," *Essays by Divers Hands*. London, 1926, pp. 139–64. Makes some useful comments on Boswell.

39. Drew, Elizabeth. "Biography," *The Enjoyment of Literature*. New York, 1935, pp. 78–108. Argues that Boswell is an "impersonal" biographer and that Johnson is a "personal" biographer.

40. Gosse, Edmund. "The Custom of Biography," *Anglo-Saxon Review*, VIII (March 1901), 195–208. Brief historical survey including Restoration and eighteenth-century biography.

41. Judson, Alexander C. "The Eighteenth-Century Lives of Edmund Spenser," *Huntington Library Quarterly*, XVI (February 1953), 161–81.

42. Lee, Sidney. "Principles of Biography," *Elizabethan and Other Essays*. Oxford, 1929, pp. 31–57. First published as a pamphlet, Cambridge, 1911. Describes briefly the uniqueness of Boswell's *Life of Johnson*.

43. Macdonald, Hugh. "The Law and Defamatory Biographies in the Seventeenth Century," *Review of English Studies*, XX (July 1944), 177–98. Discusses the many libelous biographies of political and religious controversy.

44. Pottle, Frederick A. "Notes on the Importance of Private Legal Documents for the Writing of Biography and Literary History," *Proceedings of the American Philosophical Society*, CVI (1962), 327–34. Uses some of Boswell's legal papers.

45. Stauffer, Donald A. "A Parasitical Form of Biography," *Modern Language Notes*, LV (April 1940), 289–92. Deals with biographies of historical figures used in eighteenth-century drama.

46. Wilson, F. P. "Biography," *Seventeenth Century Prose*.

Berkeley and Los Angeles, 1960, pp. 46-66. Brief treatment of Walton, Aubrey, North.

TWENTIETH CENTURY: ANTHOLOGIES WITH INTRODUCTIONS AND CRITICAL ESSAYS

47. Clifford, James L., ed. *Biography as an Art: Selected Criticism 1560–1960.* New York, 1962. Includes excerpts from the most significant Restoration and eighteenth-century critical views on biography.

48. Durling, Dwight, and William Watt, eds. *Biography: Varieties and Parallels.* New York, 1941.

49. Johnson, Edgar, ed. *A Treasury of Biography.* New York, 1941.

50. Metcalf, John C., ed. *The Stream of English Biography: Readings in Representative Biographies.* New York, 1939.

51. Pinto, Vivian de Sola, ed. *English Biography in the Seventeenth Century.* London, 1951. Contains a very useful introductory survey.

Individual Autobiographers and Biographers

JOHN AUBREY

52. Darbishire, Helen, ed. *The Early Lives of Milton.* London, 1932, pp. xxxiv-xxxix. Brief but illuminating study of Aubrey's methods.

See 19, 23, 25, 26, 29, 30, 34, 46, 47, 51, 123.

THOMAS BIRCH

53. Osborn, James M. "Thomas Birch and the *General Dictionary* (1734–1741)," *Modern Philology,* XXXVI (August 1939), 25–46.

54. Ruhe, Edward L. "Pope's Hand in Thomas Birch's Account of Gay," *Review of English Studies,* new ser., V (May 1954), 171–74.

See 37, 93.

JAMES BOSWELL

55. Bailey, John. *Dr. Johnson and His Circle*. Oxford, 1944 (rev. by L. F. Powell). Chapter on Boswell's genius as displayed in the *Life*.

56. Baldwin, Louis. "The Conversation in Boswell's *Life of Johnson*," *JEGP*, LI (October 1952), 492–506. Argues for Boswell's accuracy in reporting Johnson's conversation.

57. Barker, F. W. E. "Boswell's Record of Johnson's Table-Talk," *Papers of the Manchester Literary Club*, XLIII (1917), 93–114.

58. "Bozzies," *Eclectic Magazine*, XXIX (July 1853), 382–85. Approves Boswell's methods in the *Life*.

59. Buxton, Charles R. "Boswell's 'Life of Johnson,'" *A Politician Plays Truant: Essays on English Literature*. London, 1929, pp. 83–99. General appreciation.

60. Carlyle, Thomas. "Boswell's Life of Johnson," *Critical and Miscellaneous Essays*, ed. H. D. Traill. London, 1899, III, 62–135. First published in *Fraser's Magazine*, V (May 1832), 379–413.

61. Chapman, R. W. "Boswell's Revises of the *Life of Johnson*," *Johnson & Boswell Revised by Themselves and Others. Three Essays by David Nichol Smith, R. W. Chapman, and L. F. Powell*. Oxford, 1928, pp. 21–50.

62. Dobson, Austin. "Boswell's Predecessors and Editors," *A Paladin of Philanthropy*. London, 1899, pp. 137–72.

63. Fitzgerald, Percy. *Boswell's Autobiography*. London, 1912. Extensive study of Boswell's self-revelation in the *Life;* makes comments about Boswell's biographical method.

64. _____. *Croker's Boswell and Boswell. Studies in the "Life of Johnson."* London, 1880.

65. Haraszti, Zoltán. "The Life of Johnson," *More Books*, XII (March 1938), 99–112.

66. Hart, Edward. "The Contributions of John Nichols to Boswell's *Life of Johnson*," *PMLA*, LXVII (June 1952), 391–410. Describes Boswell's use of Nichols' *Anecdotes*.

67. Hart, Francis R. "Boswell and the Romantics: A Chapter in the History of Biographical Theory," *ELH*,

XXVII (March 1960), 44–65. Excellent study of Boswell's influence on nineteenth-century biographical theory.

68. Jack, Ian. "Two Biographers: Lockhart and Boswell," *Johnson, Boswell and Their Circle: Essays Presented to Lawrence Fitzroy Powell in Honour of His Eighty-Fourth Birthday.* Oxford, 1965, pp. 268–85. Useful comparison of biographical concerns and methods.

69. Kanki, S. "Boswell's Art as a Biographer," *Studies in English Literature* (Imperial University, Tokyo), XIII (1933), 154–60.

70. Lockhart, John Gibson. Review of Croker's edition of the *Life, Quarterly Review,* XLVI (November 1831), 1–45.

71. Macaulay, Thomas B. Review of Croker's edition of the *Life, Edinburgh Review,* LIV (August 1831), 1–38.

72. Mallory, George. *Boswell the Biographer.* London, 1912.

73. Molin, Sven E. "Boswell's Account of the Johnson-Wilkes Meeting," *Studies in English Literature,* III (Summer 1963), 307–22. Proposes that this account should be seen as "an eighteenth-century High Comedy of Manners turned into prose."

74. Morgan, Lee. "Boswell's Portrait of Goldsmith," *Studies in Honor of John C. Hodges and Alvin Thaler* (Special number of *Tennessee Studies in Literature*). Knoxville, 1961. Discusses Boswell's abuse of Goldsmith.

75. Pearson, Hesketh. "Boswell as Artist," *Cornhill Magazine,* LXXIII (December 1932), 704–11.

76. Pottle, Frederick A. "Boswell Revalued," *Literary Views: Critical and Historical Essays,* ed. Carroll Camden. Chicago, 1964, pp. 79–91. Discusses the dramatic quality and "proper emotional tone" of the *Life* and the journals.

77. _____. "The Dark Hints of Sir John Hawkins and Boswell," *New Light on Dr. Johnson: Essays on the Occasion of his 250th Birthday,* ed. F. W. Hilles. New Haven, 1959, pp. 153–62. Balanced treatment of Hawkins' and Boswell's "hints" regarding Johnson's " 'strong amorous passions.' "

78. _____. *The Literary Career of James Boswell, Esq.* Oxford, 1929.

79. ————. "The Power of Memory in Boswell and Scott," *Essays on the Eighteenth Century Presented to David Nichol Smith in Honour of His Seventieth Birthday.* Oxford, 1945, pp. 168–89. Illuminating study of Boswell's expansion of hints and clues into "imaginative reconstruction" of scenes.

80. Powell, L. F. "The Revision of Dr. Birkbeck Hill's Boswell," *Johnson and Boswell Revised by Themselves and Others.* Oxford, 1928. pp. 53–66.

81. Rait, Robert. "Boswell and Lockhart," *Essays by Divers Hands.* London 1933, pp. 105–27. Compares biographical techniques.

82. Saintsbury, George. "Some Great Biographies," *Essays in English Literature, 1875–1920.* London, 1923, I, 409–33. Includes brief treatment of the *Life.*

83. Scott, Geoffrey. *The Making of the Life of Johnson.* Vol. VI of *The Private Papers of James Boswell,* ed. Geoffrey Scott and Frederick A. Pottle. 18 vols. Mount Vernon, N. Y., 1928–1934. Outstanding study.

84. Tinker, Chauncey Brewster. "Boswell and the Art of Intimate Biography," *The Salon and English Letters.* New York, 1915, pp. 268–84. Studies Boswell's completeness; gives useful account of the reception of the *Tour.*

85. ————. *Young Boswell.* Boston, 1922. Includes chapter on the *Life,* with brief examination of some revisions.

86. Togawa, Shukotsu. "Boswell's Life of Dr. Johnson as the Theme of Biographical Study," *Studies in English Literature by the Literary Society of Japan,* XIX (1939), 1–11.

87. Vulliamy, C. E. *James Boswell.* London, 1932. Chapters on the *Life* and on Boswell's autobiography.

88. Werkmeister, Lucyle. *Jemmie Boswell and the London Daily Press, 1785–1795.* New York, 1963. Monograph which deals with reaction of the press to Boswell's *Tour* and *Life* and to the lives by Hawkins and Mrs. Piozzi.

89. Whyte, E. A. "Remarks on Boswell's Life of Johnson," *A Miscellany,* ed. E. A. and S. Whyte. London, 1797, pp. 1–42.

See 5, 17–33, 35, 38, 39, 42, 44, 47, 91, 105, 123, 126.

CHARLES BURNEY

90. Benkovitz, Miriam. "Dr. Burney's Memoirs," *Review of English Studies,* new ser., X (August 1959), 257–68. Fanny Burney's failure as her father's "memorialist."

91. Lonsdale, Roger. "Dr. Burney and the Integrity of Boswell's Quotations," *PBSA,* LIII (1959), 327–31. Supports Boswell's accuracy in quoting from Burney's letters in the *Life.*

92. Mackerness, E. D. "Dr. Burney, Biographer," *Contemporary Review,* CLXXXIX (June 1956), 352–57. Burney's contributions to Abraham Rees' *Cyclopaedia.*

JOHN DRYDEN

93. Osborn, James M. "The Earlier Biographies," *John Dryden: Some Biographical Facts and Problems.* Rev. ed., Gainesville, Fla., 1965, pp. 3–71. Excellent study of lives by Birch, Derrick, Johnson, and Malone.

EDWARD GIBBON

94. MacRobert, T. M. "Gibbon's Autobiography," *Review of English Literature,* V (January 1964), 78–83.

95. Stephen, Leslie, "Gibbon's Autobiography," *Studies of a Biographer.* New York, 1898, I, 147–87.
    See 5, 6, 8, 26, 27, 33.

OLIVER GOLDSMITH

96. Ferguson, Oliver W. "The Materials of History: Goldsmith's *Life of Nash,*" *PMLA,* LXXX (September 1965), 372–86. Illuminating study of Goldsmith's imaginative use of sources.
    See 19, 22, 23, 27, 33.

JOHN HAWKINS

97. Davis, Bertram H. *Johnson Before Boswell: A Study of Sir John Hawkins' Life of Samuel Johnson.* New Haven, 1960. Excellent attempt to correct oversimplified criticisms of Hawkins' work.

98. _____, ed. *The Life of Samuel Johnson, LL.D. by Sir John Hawkins, Knt.* New York, 1961, pp. vii–xxviii. Excellent introduction.
    See 33, 83.

SAMUEL JOHNSON

99. Abbott, John L. "Dr. Johnson and the Making of 'The Life of Father Paul Sarpi,'" *Bulletin of the John Rylands Library*, XLVIII (Spring, 1966), 255–67.

100. ————. "Dr. Johnson, Fontenelle, Le Clerc, and Six 'French' Lives," *Modern Philology*, LXIII (November 1965), 121–27. Discusses Johnson's creative use of Fontenelle and Le Clerc in brief lives written for James' *Medicinal Dictionary*.

101. Bloom, Edward. *Samuel Johnson in Grub Street*. Providence, 1957. Useful examination of Johnson's lesser known biographies.

102. Boyce, Benjamin. "Johnson's Life of Savage and Its Literary Background," *Studies in Philology*, LIII (October 1956), 576–98. Studies Johnson's use of previous accounts of Savage.

103. ————. "Samuel Johnson's Criticism of Pope in the *Life of Pope*," *Review of English Studies*, new ser., V (January 1954), 37–46. Shows Johnson's dependence on earlier biographers and critics.

104. Chapman, R. W. "Johnson's Reputation," *Johnsonian and Other Essays and Reviews*. Oxford, 1953, pp. 7–19. First part of essay deals with Johnsoniana and contemporary criticism of Johnson.

105. ————. *Two Centuries of Johnsonian Scholarship*. Glasgow, 1945. Comprehensive survey which touches on Boswell and Johnsoniana.

106. Clifford, James L. "A Biographer Looks at Doctor Johnson," *New Light on Dr. Johnson*, ed. F. W. Hilles. New Haven, 1959, pp. 121–31. First published in slightly different form in *The Columbia University Forum*, I (1958), 32–37, and included in *Academic Discourse*, ed. John J. Enck. New York, 1964, pp. 189–97.

107. ————. "Some Problems of Dr. Johnson's Obscure Middle Years," *Johnson, Boswell and Their Circle*. Oxford, 1965, pp. 99–110. Points out scarcity of detail about Johnson's life during this period.

108. Collins, J. Churton. "Dr. Johnson's 'Lives of the Poets,'"

Quarterly Review, CCVIII (January 1908), 72–97. Favorable general remarks.

109. Evans, Bergen. "Dr. Johnson's Theory of Biography," *Review of English Studies,* X (July 1934), 301–10. Useful study of Johnson's principles.

110. Greene, Donald J. "The Development of the Johnson Canon," *Restoration and Eighteenth-Century Literature: Essays in Honor of Alan Dugald McKillop,* ed. Carroll Camden. Chicago, 1963, pp. 407–27. Includes attributions of biographies to Johnson.

111. Hart, Edward. "Some New Sources of Johnson's *Lives,*" *PMLA,* LXV (December 1950), 1088–111. Argues for Johnson's indebtedness to Nichols.

112. Hazen, Allen. "Johnson's Life of Frederic Ruysch," *Bulletin of the Institute of the History of Medicine,* VIII (March 1939), 324–34.

113. _____. "Samuel Johnson and Robert James," *Bulletin of the Institute of the History of Medicine,* IV (June 1936), 455–65. Hazen's two articles attribute the lives of Ruysch, Tournefort, Aesculapius, Archagathus, Aretaeus, and Asclepedias to Johnson.

114. Hess, Walter C. "Samuel Johnson's Life of Boerhaave," *Georgetown Medical Bulletin,* XV (1962), 256–58.

115. Hilles, Frederick W. "The Making of *The Life of Pope,*" *New Light on Dr. Johnson,* ed. Frederick W. Hilles. New Haven, 1959, pp. 257–84. Important essay on the composition of this biography.

116. Keast, William R. "Johnson and 'Cibber's' *Lives of the Poets,* 1753," *Restoration and Eighteenth-Century Literature,* ed. Carroll Camden. Chicago, 1963, pp. 89–101. Discusses Shiels' use of Johnson's early biographies and other works.

117. Krutch, Joseph Wood. *Samuel Johnson.* New York, 1944. Good introduction to *Lives of the Poets.*

118. Leicester, James H. "Johnson's Life of Shenstone: Some Observations on the Sources," *Johnsonian Studies,* ed. Magdi Wahba. Cairo, 1962, pp. 189–222.

119. McAdam, Edward L., Jr. "Johnson's Lives of Sarpi, Blake, and Drake," *PMLA,* LVIII (June 1943), 466–76. Studies the sources and composition.

120. McHenry, Lawrence G. "Dr. Samuel Johnson's Medical

Biographies," *Journal of the History of Medicine,* XIV (1959), 298–310. Adds biography of Oribasius in James' *Medicinal Dictionary* to Hazen's previous ascriptions. See 112, 113.

121. _____ "Samuel Johnson's 'The Life of Dr. Sydenham,'" *Medical History,* VII (1964), 181–87.

122. Meyers, Jeffrey. "Autobiographical Reflections in Johnson's 'Life of Swift,'" *Discourse,* VIII (Winter, 1965), 37–48.

123. Raleigh, Walter. *Six Essays on Johnson.* Oxford, 1910. Contains valuable esays on Boswell and other biographers of Johnson, on pre-Johnson biography, and on the *Lives.*

124. Roberts, S. C. *Doctor Johnson and Others.* Cambridge, 1958. Discusses Johnson's early biographies, with special attention to the *Life of Savage.*

125. Stephen, Leslie. "Johnsoniana," *Studies of a Biographer.* London, 1898, I, 105–46. Review of Birkbeck Hill's *Johnsonian Miscellanies;* reveals Stephen's personal observations on Johnson's biographers and memoirists.

126. Tillinghast, Anthony J. "The Moral and Philosophical Basis of Johnson's and Boswell's Idea of Biography," *Johnsonian Studies,* ed. Magdi Wahba. Cairo, 1962, pp. 115–31. Points out influence of eighteenth-century philosophers and moralists on Johnson and Boswell.

127. Tillotson, Arthur. "Dr. Johnson and the *Life of Goldsmith,*" *Modern Language Review,* XXVIII (October 1933), 439–43. Examines reasons for Johnson's not having written a biography of Goldsmith.

128. Tracy, Clarence. "Johnson and the Art of Anecdote," *University of Toronto Quarterly,* XV (October 1945), 86–93. Excellent essay dealing with the ineffectiveness of Johnson's use of anecdotes to delineate personality.

129. Wagley, Mary Frances and Phillip F. "Comments on Samuel Johnson's Biography of Sir Thomas Browne," *Bulletin of the History of Medicine,* XXXI (1957), 318–26.

See 19—33, 35, 37, 39, 47, 93, 134, 138.

ROGER NORTH

130. Clifford, James L. "Roger North and the Art of Biography," *Restoration and Eighteenth-Century Literature,* ed. Carroll Camden. Chicago, 1963, pp. 275–85.
131. Ketton-Cramer, R. W. "Roger North," *Essays and Studies by Members of the English Association,* new ser., XII (1959), 73–86.
132. Schwoerer, Lois. "The Chronology of Roger North's Major Works," *History of Ideas News Letter,* III (October 1957), 73–78.
    See 5, 19, 22, 23, 26, 29, 30, 33, 46, 47.

THOMAS PERCY

133. Balderston, Katharine C. *The History and Sources of Percy's Memoir of Goldsmith.* Cambridge, 1926.

ALEXANDER POPE

134. Sherburn, George. "Introduction: Earlier Biographies," *The Early Career of Alexander Pope.* Oxford, 1934, pp. 1–26.

JOSEPH SPENCE

135. Dobson, Austin. "Spence's 'Anecdotes,' " *Eighteenth Century Vignettes. First Series.* London, 1892, pp. 31–37.
136. Osborn, James M., ed. Introduction to Spence's *Anecdotes.* Oxford, 1966, I, xvii–xxxiii.

JONATHAN SWIFT

137. Landa, Louis A. "Jonathan Swift," "The Critical Significance of Biographical Evidence," *English Institute Essays 1946.* New York, 1947, pp. 20–40.
138. Williams, Harold. "Swift's Early Biographers," *Pope and His Contemporaries: Essays Presented to George Sherburn,* ed. James L. Clifford and Louis A. Landa. Oxford, 1949, pp. 114–28.

IZAAK WALTON

139. Bald, R. C. "Historical Doubts Respecting Walton's *Life of Donne,*" *Essays in English Literature from*

the *Renaissance to the Victorian Age Presented to A. S. P. Woodhouse,* ed. Miller MacLure and F. W. Watt. Toronto, 1964, pp. 69–84. Challenges Walton's accuracy.

140. Bennett, R. E. "Walton's Use of Donne's Letters," *Philological Quarterly,* XVI (January 1937), 30–34.

141. McElderry, B. R., Jr. "Walton's *Lives* and Gillman's *Life of Coleridge,*" *PMLA,* LII (June 1937), 412–22. Influence of Walton on Gillman's biography.

142. Novarr, David. *The Making of Walton's "Lives."* Ithaca, 1958. Excellent study.

See 19, 21, 22, 23, 25, 26, 29, 30, 34, 46, 51, 123.

A Reading Course in Autobiography

DONALD GREENE

This is a list of suggested materials for a reading course for graduate students or advanced undergraduates in autobiographies, memoirs, diaries, and letters of eighteenth-century Britain. It is arranged very approximately in what seems to the compiler the order of importance of the items. The descriptions are intended for the student rather than the instructor. Depending on the amount of time at the student's disposal, he might be asked to acquaint himself with the first six to ten titles on the list, plus another ten or twelve chosen by him from the remaining titles. He should also be encouraged to browse—e.g., in William Matthews's *British Diaries* and *British Autobiographies, CBEL* (especially Vol. II, pp. 133–40), and Pargellis and Medley, *Bibliography of British History, 1714–1789*—for likely additions to the list. "Acquaintance" with long texts, such as Walpole's letters and Wesley's journal, would of course have to be construed as familiarity with a well-chosen selection from them.

1. John Hervey, Lord Hervey (1696–1742). *Some Materials Towards Memoirs of the Reign of George II.,* ed. Romney Sedgwick, 3 vols., 1931; there is an excellent one-volume abridgement by Sedgwick. An incomparable picture of the court and family of the irascible George and the brilliant Queen Caroline, superbly written and filled with subtle psychological insight; perhaps the closest English literature has come to Tacitus.

2. Horace Walpole, 4th Earl of Orford (1717–1797). His monumental *Correspondence,* intended for "posterity" and indispensable to both the student of literature and

the historian, is being fully edited by W. S. Lewis (Yale University Press; in progress). For general reading, however, the edition by Mrs. Paget Toynbee (*Letters*), arranged in chronological order (16 vols., 1905) is more manageable. There are several good one-volume selections, but to get the real flavor, a section at least should be read continuously.

3. Edward Gibbon (1737–1794). The *Autobiography* of the great historian is as much a classic as his *Decline and Fall*. The descriptions of his thwarted love affair ("I sighed as a lover; I obeyed as a son"), his military "career" ("The captain of the Hampshire grenadiers . . . has not been useless to the historian of the Roman Empire"), the conception and completion of the great history are unforgettable. The recent re-editing of it from various manuscripts by Dero A. Saunders (New York: Meridian Books, 1961) is recommended.

4. Lady Mary Wortley Montagu [née Pierrepont] (1689–1762). She herself invited comparison of her brilliant, witty, lively *Letters* with those of Madame de Sevigne, not without some justification. The standard edition (3 vols., 1965–1967) is by Robert Halsband. The old one-volume edition by R. Brimley Johnson in Everyman's Library is convenient.

5. David Hume (1711–1776). *My Own Life*. A tiny but perfect gem: half-a-dozen pages—his "funeral oration," he called it—in which the great skeptical philosopher and conservative historian (and master of English prose) sums up (as he is dying of cancer) his life, works, thought, character, and the spirit of the age. Included in most volumes of selections from Hume.

6. James Boswell (1740–1795). The publication of the *Journal* which he maintained from adolescence is in progress (McGraw-Hill). The *London Journal, 1762–63,* a bestseller when it was first printed in 1950, is probably still the best introduction for the general reader. It might be supplemented by the *Journal of a Tour to the Hebrides with Samuel Johnson, LL.D.,* Boswell's masterpiece, and by some reading in the depressing later journals (as yet available only in the privately-printed *Private Papers from Malahide Castle,* 1928–1934), which show Boswell

fighting a losing battle with his alcoholism and sexual compulsion.

7. Jonathan Swift (1667–1745). The *Journal to Stella,* Swift's intimate diary of the exciting period in London at the end of Queen Anne's reign when he acted as "minister of propaganda" to the Tory government of Harley and Bolingbroke. The standard edition is by Sir Harold Williams, 2 vols., 1948.

8. Frances (Fanny) Burney, later Mme. d'Arblay (1752–1840). *Diaries.* The most attractive production of the sly and demure but clever Fanny, who achieved unexpected fame with her early novel *Evelina.* The one-volume selection in Everyman's Library, ed. Lewis Gibbs, is good. Students may wish to read further in the *Early Diary, 1768–72,* ed. A. R. Ellis, 2 vols., 1889, and the *Diary and Letters,* ed. Austin Dobson, 6 vols., 1904. Fanny heavily edited her papers, in order to conceal scandals in the Burney family and the like; they are laboriously being restored to their original form by Professor Joyce Hemlow of McGill University and a team of assistants.

9. Joseph Spence (1699–1768). *Anecdotes, Observations, and Characters, of Books and Men. Collected from the Conversation of Mr. Pope, and Other Eminent Persons.* The great "table talk" of the 18th century, as Selden's is of the 17th and Coleridge's and Rogers's of the 19th. Amusing and a valuable primary source for eighteenth-century literary history. The title above is that of S. W. Singer's edition, 1820; a monumental new edition (1966) by James M. Osborn is the standard one.

10. Hester Lynch Piozzi (earlier Mrs. Thrale; née Salusbury) (1741–1821). *Thraliana.* Ed. Katharine C. Balderston, 2 vols., 1942 (2nd ed., 1951). The diary and commonplace book of a clever, learned, and generally remarkable woman who had a somewhat remarkable life, as the intimate of Dr. Johnson and the center of a great scandal (as a widow of forty she fell in love with and married an Italian musician!).

11. John Wesley (1703–1791). *Journal.* Ed. N. Curnock, 8 vols.; many other editions and selections. A very great work—theologically and historically considered to be ranked with St. Augustine's *Confessions.* Every serious

student of the eighteenth century should read in it at some time or other.

12. John Thomas Smith (1766–1833). *Nollekens and His Times* (2 vols., 1828; later reprints). This "life" of the greatest English sculptor of the 18th century may be placed here because (like Boswell's *Johnson*) it is as much autobiography as biography. Equally self-revelatory with Boswell's *Life,* and second only to it (if that) as entertainment. A wonderful book that too few modern students know. Smith's later *A Book for a Rainy Day, or Recollections of the Events of the Last Sixty-Six Years* (1845) is somewhat late for this period, but is almost as good an example of Smith's amusing vein as the Nollekens. Smith was trained as an artist and became Keeper of the Prints in the British Museum.

13. Colley Cibber (1671–1757). *An Apology for the Life of Mr. Colley Cibber, Comedian* (first published 1740; later editions, including one in Everyman's). The last word in the title is the operative one in describing the Poet Laureate of George II and the hero of the *Dunciad.* Colley was by no means the dunce Pope suggests, but a fine comic actor and clever theater manager. Amusing, and an important document in the history of the English stage.

14. Philip Dormer Stanhope, 4th Earl of Chesterfield (1694–1773). The *Letters to His Son,* intended to educate his illegitimate son in "the Graces"—they failed conspicuously to do so—are a strange performance. Written in elegant prose, they teach, according to Chesterfield's enemy, Johnson, "the manners of a dancing master and the morals of a whore." Nevertheless they give a vivid picture of life at the *haut ton* level.

15. Thomas Gray (1716–1771). See comment below.

16. William Cowper (1731–1800). Their *Letters* used to be regarded as compulsory reading for all students of the period, perhaps because Gray and Cowper were regarded as "pre-Romantics." The letters now seem a little too precious and self-conscious for modern tastes, by comparison with, say, Lady Mary Wortley Montagu's; but they are nevertheless very good. Cowper's short *Memoir,* in which he attempts to trace the history of his despondency,

which later became (or was classed as) madness, is of great psychological interest.

17. Alexander ("Jupiter") Carlyle (1722–1805). The *Autobiography* of this witty and intellectual Scottish clergyman gives a wonderfully vivid picture of life in Edinburgh during the "golden age" of intellectual life there.

18. Sarah Churchill (née Jennings), Duchess of Marlborough (1660–1744). Her memoirs (*An Account of the Conduct of the Dowager Duchess of Marlborough,* 1742), prepared shortly before the death of the indomitable woman who, with her husband the great Duke, ran England during the first part of Queen Anne's reign, are as exuberant as one might expect from the co-founder of the Churchill family's fortunes. She spares her contemporaries, including William III, Queen Mary, and Queen Anne, nothing.

19. Mary Cowper (née Clavering), Countess Cowper (1684–1724). The *Diary* of this distant relation of the poet, wife of George I's Lord Chancellor, is entertaining in its acid accounts of her contemporaries at court and her husband's political rivals. A valuable picture of the establishment of the Whig regime in politics that lasted throughout the century.

20. Samuel Johnson (1709–1784). His short fragment of an autobiography, included in *Diaries, Prayers, and Annals* (Volume I of the Yale Edition of the *Works of Samuel Johnson,* 1958) is very fine. The rest of the volume is at least worth dipping into; it tells much that will not be found in Boswell about Johnson's inner life. Johnson's *Letters* (ed. R. W. Chapman, 3 vols., 1952) tend to be underrated; they are often lively, humorous, and enjoyable.

21. Henry Fielding (1707–1754). His *Journal of a Voyage to Lisbon* (ed. Harold Pagliaro, 1963), written by a sick man undertaking the journey for the sake of his health, is a vividly written record of gloom, annoyance, and frustration (Fielding died soon after his arrival at Lisbon). But like everything by Fielding, very readable, and of psychological interest.

22. James Woodforde (1758–1802). *The Diary of a Country Parson,* ed. J. B. Beresford, 1924–1931. A detailed ac-

count of rural life of the period by a phlegmatic, self-indulgent, but not unintelligent or unobservant Anglican clergyman.

23. William Cole (1714–1782). *The Bletchley Diary, 1765–67.* A different type of clergyman, an intellectual, antiquarian researcher, friend and correspondent of Horace Walpole.

24. Thomas Hearne (1678–1735). Librarian, antiquarian, and ferocious Jacobite sympathizer. His *Remarks and Collections* (Oxford Historical Society, 11 vols.) picture a scholar's life at Oxford in the early part of the century. His jaundiced comments on all the political and academic notables of the day make amusing reading. There is a one-volume abridgement, ed. John Buchanan–Brown, 1966.

25. Richard Cumberland (1732–1811). *Memoirs,* London, 1806. A lively, conceited autobiography by a practitioner of the "sentimental comedy" and government "placeman." Amusing anecdotes of his grandfather, the great Richard Bentley, and the eighteenth-century theatrical scene.

26. John Perceval, 1st Earl of Egmont. *Diary, 1730–1747,* Historical MSS Commission Reports, 1920–1923. See comment below.

27. George Bubb Dodington, Lord Melcombe (1691–1762). *The Political Diary,* ed. John Carswell and L. A. Dralle, 1966. Two of the important political diaries of the time. Dodington's is a particularly lively self-revelation by an unabashed but often frustrated office-seeker.

28. Dudley Ryder (1691–1756). Later Attorney-General and Lord Chief Justice of England. The *Diary* of his life as a law student, 1715–1716 (including much about contemporary social and theatrical life in London) was edited by William Matthews, 1939.

29. Mary Delany (formerly Mrs. Pendarves; née Granville) (1700–1788). *Autobiography and Correspondence,* ed. S. C. Woolsey, 1879. A woman of aristocratic family, who after an early unhappy marriage married Swift's friend Dean Delany; later a close friend of George III's queen, Charlotte; reminiscences of literary, social, and court life.

30. Richard Watson, Bishop of Llandaff (1737–1816). Scien-

tist and divine (successively professor of chemistry and divinity at Cambridge), he remained bishop of a small and poor Welsh diocese (which he seldom visited) because of his radical political views. *Anecdotes of the Life of Richard Watson, D.D. Written by Himself*, 1817.

31. Laetitia Pilkington (1712–1750). Described by *DNB* as "adventuress"; friend of Swift. *Memoirs*, 1748.

32. George Anne Bellamy (?1731–1788). Actress. *Apology*, 1785.

33. Charlotte Charke (d. ca. 1760). Daughter of Colley Cibber; actress and theatrical hanger-on. *Narrative of the Life . . . Written by Herself*, 1755. Examples of *chroniques scandaleuses* in autobiographical form by ladies of greater or less disreputability, a popular genre during the century (cf. the Memoirs of Lady Vane in Smollett's *Peregrine Pickle*). They soon become tiresome; Laetitia Pilkington's is the best.

34. William Hickey (1749–1809). *Memoirs*, ed. Peter Quennell, 1962. Sexual and alcoholic escapades; life in India and the Far East. Like Boswell, Hickey is fond of contemplating his own deviltry.

35. Laetitia Matilda Hawkins (ca. 1760–1835). The garrulous and admiring daughter of Sir John Hawkins, magistrate, musicologist, friend and biographer of Johnson. *Anecdotes, Biographical Sketches, and Memoirs*, 1822; *Memoirs, Anecdotes, Facts, and Opinions*, 2 vols., 1824.

36. John Byrom (1692–1763). Poet, hymn-writer, inventor of a shorthand system, Jacobite, Fellow of the Royal Society. *Private Journal and Literary Remains*, ed. R. Parkinson, 4 vols., Manchester, 1854-1857. A fine, too much neglected "religious diary" (with other things as well).

37. Charles Burney, Mus. D. (1726–1814). Fanny's father, an important pioneer musicologist. His *The Present State of Music in France and Italy*, 1771, and *in Germany, the Netherlands*, etc., 1773, as well as being primary documents for the history of eighteenth-century music, are enjoyable travel diaries.

Notes

The documentary styles of the individual authors have been generally preserved, with minimal editing. The following cue title applies to all the essays:
Life: James Boswell. *The Life of Samuel Johnson, LL.D.* Ed. G. B. Hill, rev. L. F. Powell. 6 vols. Oxford, 1934–1950.

DAGHLIAN: *Introduction*

1. Readers will be familiar with works such as Frederick A. Pottle, "The Power of Memory in Boswell and Scott" in *Essays on the Eighteenth Century Presented to David Nichol Smith,* Oxford, 1945 [reissued New York 1963]; and Bertrand H. Bronson, "Boswell's Boswell" in *Johnson Agonistes and Other Essays,* Cambridge, 1946.

2. *The Last Days of Hitler,* London & New York, 1947; *The Last Battle,* New York, 1966.

RADER: *Literary Form in Factual Narrative: The Example of Boswell's* Johnson

1. Many of the concepts articulated here were first developed in a graduate seminar which I gave in the spring of 1964 at the University of California, Berkeley. I wish to acknowledge my debt to the students in that seminar, particularly Gerry Brookes, William Chace, Peter Collier, Robert Hirst, John Hunter, and James Johnson. Since the lecture was written, it has benefited from the criticisms of Paul Alkon, Bertrand H. Bronson, James L. Clifford, Philip B. Daghlian, and Frederick A. Pottle, to all of whom I am grateful.

2. Donald A. Stauffer, *The Art of Biography in Eighteenth-Century England* (Princeton, 1941), pp. 445–46.

3. John A. Garraty, *The Nature of Biography* (New York, 1964), pp. 26, 95.

4. Joseph Wood Krutch, *Samuel Johnson* (New York, 1941), p. 386.

5. George Mallory, *Boswell the Biographer* (London, 1912), pp. 293, 278, 271, 281.

6. Professor Pottle has put the case for Boswell's imaginative creativity more explicitly (and accurately, I believe) than any other critic. See Frederick A. Pottle, *James Boswell: The Earlier Years, 1740–1769* (New York, 1966), pp. 87–90, and an earlier article, "The Life of Boswell," *Yale Review*, XXV (Spring, 1946), 445–60.

7. *Life*, II, 299.

8. Hester Lynch Piozzi, *Anecdotes of the Late Samuel Johnson, LL.D.*, ed. G. B. Hill in *Johnsonian Miscellanies* (Oxford, 1897), I, 224.

9. Sir John Hawkins, *The Life of Dr. Samuel Johnson*, in *The Works of Samuel Johnson* (London, 1787), I, 11.

10. *Life of Johnson*, II, 76–77.

11. James L. Clifford, *Hester Lynch Piozzi (Mrs. Thrale)* (Oxford, 1941), p. 357: "Boswell's superiority over his rival biographers . . . lies not only in the completeness of his picture of Johnson, but also in the significant definition, the delicate shading, and the general coherence of his portrait. He justifies himself as a creative artist."

12. *Life*, I, 372–77.

13. Philip B. Daghlian, "Samuel Johnson," in *The Familiar Letter in the Eighteenth Century*, ed. Howard Anderson *et al.* (Lawrence, Kansas, 1966), pp. 109, 128.

14. *Life*, IV, 320.

15. *Life*, III, 323–24.

16. *Life*, IV, 10; IV, 183.

17. *Life*, III, 64–79.

18. The conception of a comic action offered here is obviously indebted to R. S. Crane's "The Concept of Plot and the Plot of *Tom Jones*," reprinted in *Critics and Criticism*, abridged ed. (Chicago, 1957), pp. 82–83.

19. *Life*, II, 106–107.

20. *Life*, IV, 108–109.

21. *Life*, I, 30.

22. Hallam Tennyson's attempt to sustain an attitude of reverence in his *Memoir* of his father is largely unsuccessful because Tennyson's character is consistently presented as with-

out defect and because Hallam's represented reverential attitude has no adequate correlative in the facts as presented.

23. In "Of Tragedy."

24. I am well aware that all readers of Boswell do not admire Johnson consistently throughout the book, and that some do not admire him at all. This does not alter the fact that, formally speaking, Johnson is always presented so as to sustain the effect of admiration. That Boswell should fail of his intended effect in some passages or with some readers is no more evidence of a lack of consistent artistry than that Wordsworth, for example, should often fail of his effect in similar ways. The strong wine that Boswell offers can sometimes be fully savored only if the reader has the capacity to take the same disinterested delight in the powers of human nature that Boswell does. But that Boswell in fact achieves his effect with most readers the unique position of his book in literary history testifies.

25. *Life,* I, 468.

26. *Life,* III, 337.

27. Thomas Carlyle, "Boswell's Life of Johnson," *Critical and Miscellaneous Essays* (London, 1899), III, 80.

28. *Life,* I, 472.

29. "Biography," *Critical and Miscellaneous Essays* (London, 1899), III, 56.

30. *Life,* II, 433.

31. Like the description of Gibbon's *Decline and Fall* above, this statement is intended to articulate the large formal principle which governs the work.

GREENE: *The Uses of Autobiography in the Eighteenth Century*

1. Samuel Johnson, *Diaries, Prayers, Annals,* ed. E. L. McAdam, Jr. with Donald and Mary Hyde (New Haven, 1958), pp. 3, 8–9 (*The Yale Edition of the Works of Samuel Johnson,* Vol. I).

2. *Life,* IV, 284–85.

3. Johnson in his old age wrote a good deal of a translation of Sallust, which is still extant in manuscript.

4. In fact, the *Edinburgh Review's* notice (VII [January, 1806], 436–41) of the first publication of the fragment takes a

devastatingly superior attitude toward these details. *The Wellesley Index of Victorian Periodical Literature*, I, 438, is uncertain whether the reviewer was Lord Brougham or Lord Jeffrey.

5. For recent recognition of Johnson's anticipation of much "modern" psychological insight, see Kathleen Grange, "Samuel Johnson's Account of Certain Psychoanalytic Concepts," *Journal of Nervous and Mental Disease*, CXXXV (August, 1962), 93–98, and "Dr. Samuel Johnson's Account of a Schizophrenic Illness in *Rasselas*," *Medical History*, VI (1962), 162–68. The first-named article is reprinted in D. J. Greene, ed., *Samuel Johnson: A Collection of Critical Essays* (Englewood Cliffs, N. J., 1965).

6. Meyer A. Zeligs, *Friendship and Fratricide: An Analysis of Whittaker Chambers and Alger Hiss* (New York, 1967); Sigmund Freud and William C. Bullitt, *Thomas Woodrow Wilson . . . A Psychological Study* (Boston, 1967).

7. William Hickey, *Memoirs,* ed. Peter Quennell (London, 1960).

8. If history is a tree, Namier once told Arnold Toynbee, he, Namier, was concerned with the leaves. "The single leaves, which are the realities with which Lewis [Namier] sought to operate, are the individual human beings whose innumerable and intricately interwoven relations with each other produce the tangled fabric of history": Arnold Toynbee, "Sir Lewis Namier," *Harper's*, May, 1967, p. 59 (an extract from Toynbee's book, *Acquaintances* [London, 1967]).

9. Lytton Strachey, Preface to *Eminent Victorians*.

10. *The Political Diary of George Bubb Dodington* (Oxford, 1965).

11. Morris, p. 223.

12. Morris, p. 39.

13. Morris, p. 82.

CLIFFORD: *How Much Should a Biographer Tell? Some Eighteenth-Century Views*

1. *Saturday Review,* 21 January 1967, p. 18; *Newsweek,* 26 December, 1966.

2. The Earl of Birkenhead, *Daily Telegraph* [London] 23 May 1966, p. 14.

3. Lord Chandos, "O Tempora, O Moran!" *Spectator*, 27 May 1966, p. 657.

4. *Ibid:* and letter from Lord Normanbrook, *Times* [London] 24 May 1966, p. 13.

5. *Daily Mirror* [London] 27 April 1966 (front page).

6. Pertinax in the *British Medical Journal*, quoted by John Prince in *Daily Telegraph*, 29 April 1966, p. 17. See also letters by H. A. Williams and Denis Brogan, *Times*, 27 April, p. 13 and 2 May, p. 11.

7. Denis Brogan, loc. cit.; and Malcolm Elwin, 16 May 1966.

8. Editorial, *New York Times*, 28 July 1966; and article, 26 May 1967, pp. 1, 28.

9. *Monthly Review*, XIX (October 1758), 386. The ascription of authorship is given in Benjamin Nangle, *The Monthly Review, First Series* (1934), p. 147.

10. See, for example, William Beckford's *Biographical Memoirs of Extraordinary Painters* (1780), written when he was only seventeen, a somewhat heavy-handed satire on Continental biographical works. In places it burlesques the stress on trivial matters. See also references to Peter Pindar (notes 41 and 50 below).

11. 20 April 1716.

12. From "An Account of the Life and Writings of Mr. Abraham Cowley," in *Works* (1668), addressed to Martin Clifford.

13. *Aubrey's Brief Lives*, ed. Andrew Clark (1898), I, 10-11 [15 June 1680].

14. See *Biography as an Art: Selected Criticism, 1560–1960*, ed. James L. Clifford (1962), pp. 27–37. The manuscript is now in the library of St. John's College, Cambridge.

15. Roger North, *Lives of the Norths* (1826), I, 154.

16. *Ibid*, I, 91–93; II, 167–68; II, 366.

17. See my "Roger North and the Art of Biography" in *Restoration and Eighteenth-Century Literature: Essays in Honor of Alan D. McKillop* (1963), pp. 275–81.

18. B. M. Add. MS. 32,509 f9v.

19. I am indebted to Mr. Peter Millard of Linacre College, Oxford, for this and other comments relative to North's manuscripts. Mr. Millard is engaged in editing Roger North's life of his brother John, and has been making a careful study of all of the North biographical manuscripts.

20. For a typical approach to biography as instruction, see Oliver Goldsmith's Preface to *Plutarch's Lives* (*Works,* ed. Arthur Friedman [1966], V, 226–28). Also, see "On Biography," *Lady's Magazine,* XVIII (August 1787), 425.

21. I owe this suggestion to Professor Edward Ruhe. To be sure Defoe is writing fiction, but the pretence is that he is merely the editor of a memoir.

22. Of course, there were a few revealing short biographical pieces, such as the account of John Hall (1627–56) by John Davies of Kidwelly, in Hall's posthumous translation of *Hierocles upon the Golden Verses of Pythagoras* (1657). I owe this to Professor William R. Parker. Thanks are also due to Mr. Terry Belanger for other help with the documentation.

23. V. 301; 73–74.

24. Cf. David Mallet, *Life of Bacon* (1740). William Oldys, *Memoirs of Mrs. Anne Oldfield* (1741), p. 28; William Ayre, *Memoirs of the Life and Writings of Alexander Pope* (1745). Mallet had stressed that a biographer "is fairly to record the faults as well as the good qualities, the failings as well as the perfections, of the Dead"; and Oldys insisted that it "is the Duty of an Historian to speak the Truth, as far as it comes to his Knowledge."

25. For the influence of contemporary philosophy on biography, see Anthony J. Tillinghast, "The Moral and Philosophical Basis of Johnson's and Boswell's Idea of Biography." *Johnsonian Studies,* ed. Magdi Wahba (Cairo, 1962), pp. 115–31.

26. Some standard analysis of this shift of sensibility may be found in W. J. Bate, *From Classic to Romantic* (1946); Meyer H. Abrams, *The Mirror and the Lamp* (1953); Northrop Frye, "Towards Defining an Age of Sensibility," *ELH,* XXIII (June 1956), 144–52.

27. The best recent analysis of Johnson as a biographer is that by John Butt, in *Biography in the Hands of Walton, Johnson, and Boswell* (University of California, Los Angeles, 1966), pp. 19–32.

28. See Harold Nicolson, *The Development of English Biography* (1927), pp. 76, 84–85; Edmund Bergler, "Samuel Johnson's 'Life of the Poet Richard Savage'—a Paradigm for a Type," *American Imago,* IV (December 1947), 42–63.

29. William Oldys in his *Life of Sir Walter Raleigh* (1736), p. vii, when giving a light anecdote from Raleigh's Oxford

days, explained that "a great Discovery of Genius may be made through a small and sudden Repartee."

30. Bodleian Library, MS. Malone 30.

31. *Life*, III, 154–55 [17 September 1777].

32. *Lives of the Poets*, ed. G. B. Hill (1905), II, 116.

33. William Mason, *Memoirs of the Life and Writings of Mr. Gray* (1775), II, 40.

34. In the Yale Boswell Collection. For other omissions mentioned see: Donald and Mary Hyde, "Dr. Johnson's Second Wife," *New Light on Dr. Johnson*, ed. F. W. Hilles (1959) pp. 133–51; J. L. Clifford, *Young Sam Johnson* (1955) pp. 142–43, 314–17; Boswell's original manuscript of *Life* (Yale Collection).

35. *Boswell's Journal of a Tour to the Hebrides with Samuel Johnson, LL.D Now First Published from the Original Manuscript*, ed. F. A. Pottle and C. H. Bennett (1936), pp. 114–15; *Life*, V, 147–49.

36. The remarks about Langton and about Captain Brodie were in the original manuscript version of the *Life*. The omission of the remarks about Percy and Reynolds is discussed by F. A. Pottle in *The Literary Career of James Boswell* (1929), pp. 150–51.

37. *Letters of James Boswell*, ed. C. B. Tinker (1924), II, 422.

38. *Life*, V, 415–16.

39. *Correspondence*, ed. Toynbee, XIII, 337 [6 October 1785].

40. John Rylands Library MS. 544,5 (31 December 1785) in a letter to Mrs. Piozzi in Italy.

41. Peter Pindar, *A Poetical and Congratulatory Epistle to James Boswell* [1785], 3d ed. (1796), p. 9.

42. B. R. McElderry Jr., *N&Q*, July 1962, p. 268.

43. Manuscript in my possession, unsigned. Partly quoted by Katherine G. Hornbeak in *The Age of Johnson* (1949), p. 361. A signed letter, containing some of the comments is in the John Rylands Library, MS. 551,2. See my *Hester Lynch Piozzi (Mrs. Thrale)* (1941), pp. 272–73. The unsigned version may have been fuller because it was a first draft.

44. *Monthly Review*, LXXIV (April 1786), 277–82; B. C. Nangle, *Monthly Review, First Series* (1934), p. 65.

45. Sir William Forbes, *Life of Beattie* (1806), II, 184.

46. W. Roberts, *Memoirs of Hannah More* (1834), II, 16.

47. *Monthly Review,* LXXIV (May 1786), 373–74; Nangle, p. 209.

48. *The English Review,* VII (April 1786), 254.

49. *New Annual Register for 1786* (1787), 263; also *Monthly Review,* LXXIV (May 1786), 373–74.

50. Peter Pindar, *Bozzy & Piozzi: or the British Biographers A Town Eclogue* [1786], 9th ed. (1788), pp. 49–50.

51. *The English Review,* VII (June 1786).

52. *Winter Evenings,* 2nd ed. (1790), I, 105. Knox in his earlier essay "Cursory Thoughts on Biography" in *Essays Moral and Literary* (1782), II, 48–52, has nothing significant to say about the main problems.

53. See B. R. McElderry [note 42], who quotes from Montagu Papers in the Huntington Library. Mrs. Alison wrote on 16 March 1791. Even among Boswell's friends there had been some reluctance to allow him to use Johnson's personal letters to them. Dr. Taylor refused to allow him to use his, and William Bowles wrote to Boswell, 14 November 1787, "there is not a single passage in any of my letters that can assist towards the knowledge of *Life or opinions." (Fettercairn Catalogue* [1936], p. 21.) Revealing examples of the kinds of pressure for censorship exerted on Boswell by his friends may be found in Marshall Waingrow's forthcoming *The Correspondence and Other Papers of James Boswell Relating to the Making of the "Life of Johnson"* (Yale Research Edition).

54. *Life,* V, 572; *Fettercairn Catalogue,* Nos. 792–94, 985–86, 1288–89, 1300–1, 1453.

55. Anna Laetitia Barbauld, *Works,* ed. Lucy Aiken (1825), II, 157–58. (written at Hampstead, May 1791).

56. Robert Anderson, *Life of Samuel Johnson,* 3d ed. (1815), p. 6.

57. *Ibid.*

58. Stephen Spender, in "How Much Should a Biographer Tell?" *SR,* XLVII (25 January 1964), 16–19, suggests that the biographer thought of himself as a kind of filter. Having been entrusted by the family with a mass of surviving documents and papers, he had to decide what could properly be made public, in the interests both of his hero and the family.

59. *Monthly Review,* n.s. VII (January 1792), 3–4; Nangle, *Second Series* (1955), p. 92.

60. Samuel Whyte, *Miscellanea Nova* (1800), pp. vi–vii.

61. As Spender [note 58] puts it, Boswell says he gives Johnson "warts and all," but "warts are not the same as intestines."

62. *Daily Telegraph* [London] 29 April, 1966, p. 16.

63. A writer in *Public Characters of 1798* (1798) [Preface] stresses the difficulties of a contemporary biographer, "who is restrained, by the extreme delicacy of his undertaking, from giving the finishing stroke to his delineations of character, whose incomplete materials prevent him from deducing general and important conclusions in their proper latitude, and, in many cases, from discriminating between hypocrisy and sincerity."